MW00441963

WORKING
Girls

MORE BY
TRIXIE MATTEL & KATYA

Trixie and Katya's
Guide to Modern
Womanhood ↖

It's a New York Times
Bestseller

WORKING
Girls

Trixie & Katya's
Guide to **Professional**
Womanhood

TRIXIE MATTEL &
KATYA ZAMOLODCHIKOVA

PLUME

PLUME

An imprint of Penguin Random House LLC
penguinrandomhouse.com

Copyright © 2022 by Brian Michael Firkus and Brian Joseph McCook
Penguin supports copyright. Copyright fuels creativity, encourages diverse
voices, promotes free speech, and creates a vibrant culture. Thank you for
buying an authorized edition of this book and for complying with copyright laws
by not reproducing, scanning, or distributing any part of it in any form without
permission. You are supporting writers and allowing Penguin to continue to
publish books for every reader.

PLUME and P colophon are registered trademarks of Penguin Random House LLC

Photographs by Albert Sanchez and Pedro Zalba

LIBRARY OF CONGRESS CATALOGING-IN-PUBLICATION DATA
has been applied for.

ISBN 9780593186114 (hardcover)
ISBN 9780593186121 (ebook)

Printed in the United States of America

1st Printing

BOOK DESIGN BY SHANNON NICOLE PLUNKETT

This book is dedicated to all the divas
who slay and serve and work the
house down boots, hunty

CONTENTS

PART TWO

THRIVING AT WORK

PART THREE

LEAVING YOUR JOB / CAREER TRANSITIONS

WORKING
Girls

PART ONE

GETTING

THE JOB

CAREER APTITUDE TEST

BY KATYA

Congratulations on taking the first step on your journey toward complete and total mastery of professional nirvana. If you've purchased this book, I can only assume that you are a plucky young blonde named Jessica ready to claw your way up the corporate ladder, armed with a can-do spirit; firm, tanned thighs; and a pair of big, heavy naturals. I could also assume you're a newly divorced mother of two, a busty dame in your late forties named Gina, looking to launch your second act after finally having unburdened yourself of that deadbeat husband, Ric. Well done, Gina, and welcome home. Then again, you could be someone else entirely, perhaps someone from the future named Beth or Bethany or Elizabeth, and you've found this dusty tome wedged in the rubble of a blown-out Barnes & Noble bathroom, and that's fine too. Listen, Beth, the important thing is that you are here, and you're ready to do the work.

This book will serve as your road map of the daunting landscape of five-lane freeways that populate the endlessly winding and weaving labyrinth of the modern professional world. Unlike the freeway, however, in the professional world there are no signs to guide you to a graceful exit or to indicate a change of lane, but that's where we come in: to extend a petite and perfectly manicured helping hand. Grab on tight, don't let go, and when you're done, please return the hand to the mannequin in the American Eagle on the first level of the Greendale Mall.

This is a guide meant to serve you no matter where you might find yourself positioned in the rat race, from interviewing for your first job all the way to basking in the golden glow of retirement. And you can rest assured, beyond any shadow of a doubt, that you're about to receive not only the most sound and reasonable career advice of all time but also the most innovative and cutting-edge techniques and practices for professional advancement, from two trustworthy titans of talent. Of course I'm referring to myself and Trixie, who also happen to be two out-of-touch drag queens whose combined professional experience is less than that of the average college teen and dates back to well over a decade ago. But consider this: The benefits of a fresh and unconventional point of view can be invaluable, just as in the 1980s, when beleaguered homicide detectives were forced to think outside the box and hire psychics and Reiki masters. They might not have helped to solve any cases per se, but these collaborations did usher in an important paradigm shift: We now more fully understand how to harness the energy of passed loved ones to help detectives explore each other's bodies. So, please, allow us to blindly guide you off the cliff, fake hand in real one—but before we get into the whole rigmarole of working, jobs, blah blah blah, there's one thing we need to figure out: Who exactly are you?

Back in high school there was a guidance counselor named Mrs. Liljestrand whose job was to help students figure out what to do after graduation. She was an enigmatic figure, as she seemed to work only about two hours a week but somehow owned several BMWs. She also had the strange habit of changing the pronunciation of her own last name every couple of months. Needless to say, I was in love with her, and one day, after months of trying, I finally managed to catch her in the office. I asked her, "Why do we only have two options after high school? It seems strange and kind of depressing that I must either become a janitor or go to Harvard. Is there no third option?" She took a long drag of her Cuban cigarillo, blew it at the glass of the unopened window, slowly craned her neck back at me, and after a long, exasperated sigh said, "Listen, honey, if I had all the answers, then I'd know why the back seats of all my Beamers are filled with dead birds." I was stunned silent until she threw a mop at me and said, "Get the fuck out of here; you'll never get into Harvard." Like most mysterious oracles, she was weird, and she was right.

One of the most fascinating things about people is that they are all made up of so many different things. And I'm not talking just about blood, phlegm, bile, and pizzazz. I'm talking about the things that make you *You* and the other stuff that makes me *Me*, not to mention the entirely different sack of whatever that makes Shakira *Shakira*. Psychiatrists say that each person on this planet is unique, which to me sounds like a bunch of malarkey. Next thing you know, they'll say the moon isn't made of cheese and Earth spins around like a giant basketball. There are nearly 225,000 people currently living on God's green flat Earth, and you're gonna tell me that they are all one of a kind? Well, I think the more than sixty-five documented sets of identical twins would beg to differ, which is hard for them to do since they look exactly the same.

But enough about science. This book is about the real world, and in the real world we don't drive microscopes and drink out of test tubes. We do stuff for money, and that's called work.

To get you on the right path, we need to identify just what kind of stuff it is that you like and what types of things you could be good at. You've probably heard of aptitude tests before, and maybe you've even taken one. They usually consist of a series of questions about your skills, preferences, and working style— and they are not to be confused with the slightly different Alptitude test, which simply proves whether a mountain is European. The results are designed to indicate which fields you are suited to based on your answers.

Unfortunately, there are many problems with these tests. First of all, they are far too long and don't require any blood or urine samples, which too often yields a boring and inaccurate assessment. Second, the jobs they recommend are often obsolete, illegal, or just plain yucky. Physician? What's the point when we already have doctors? That's why I came up with this ingenious, foolproof, all-encompassing aptitude test for the modern working girl.

QUESTION 1:

Choose the activity that appeals to you the most:

A: Solving problems with oldies

B: Vehicular manslaughter

C: Feeling up on people's legs

D: Looking at bones

QUESTION 2:

Which smell reminds you the most of home?

A: Charred fish

B: Marinated mushrooms

C: Hot, wet air

D: Greased leather

QUESTION 3:

Which location do you find it impossible to make love in?

A: The ocean

B: An Irish bog

C: A vintage pioneer wagon

D: Germany

QUESTION 4:

Which body of water do you find the most alluring?

A: The Petersons' aboveground pool

B: The Dead Sea

C: The Gulf of Mexico

D: The fish tank in the dentist's waiting room

QUESTION 5:

How many different species of animals have you touched with both hands?

A: 0

B: 1–5

C: 10–100

D: Too many to count

QUESTION 6:

Which of the following is Academy Award–nominated actress Ellen Burstyn's real name?

A: Edith Megan Guggenheim

B: Edna Rae Gillooly

C: Eden Ruth Friedman

D: Helen Bursting

QUESTION 7:

If Stephanie is traveling westward at twenty-five miles per hour for a job interview at 4:00 p.m. and she leaves her house at 2:00 p.m. but her car runs out of gas halfway to her destination, how does that make you feel?

A: Angry

B: Buoyed

C: Hopeful

D: Despondent

QUESTION 8:

What did you have for lunch today?

A: Continental breakfast in the lobby

B: Meals on Wheels

C: Steak Diane

D: A big bowl of Ma's gravy

QUESTION 9:

What concession do you buy at the movies?

A: Popcorn

B: Jujubes

C: Raisinets

D: Cobb salad, buttery dressing on the side

QUESTION 10:

You discover that your boss is having an affair with his executive assistant. Do you:

A: Use this information as leverage to get a raise?

B: Threaten to change him from a rooster to a hen with a shotgun?

C: Casually insert yourself as the third amorous partner?

D: Post an anonymous report to the work bulletin board?

QUESTION 11:

Which scenario do you find the most unpleasant?

A: Cutting your hair very short

B: Being married to an actor

C: Giving birth to the spawn of Satan

D: Listening to stand-up comedy

QUESTION 12:

It's 10:00 p.m. on a weeknight and you hear a knock at the door. Who's likely to be there?

A: Kim Cattrall

B: A large chunk of meteorite

C: A tall religious zealot

D: A steaming jar of Ma's gravy

IF YOU GOT:

Mostly As: You should be a medical technician.

Mostly Bs: You should be an after-hours DJ.

Mostly Cs: You may qualify for 0 percent APR financing.

Mostly Ds: You are a cardiac surgeon at Boston Medical, and you were due in surgery more than four hours ago! Everyone is really worried; please get to the operating room at once, Doctor. Time is running out, and there's one thing you need to know about the patient. It's . . . your son, Jeremy. For Christ's sake, hurry!

To Do:

Pick out urn
for Jeremy.

WHAT KIND OF JOB DO YOU WANT?

Service Work Edition

BY TRIXIE & KATYA

Are you a fierce fucking diva who lives to serve? Well, take a number, bitch, and welcome to the club, because we are too. Most of the jobs we've worked have been in the service industry, which probably had something to do with the fact that we became such fierce divas who can't stop serving. Before we run down the list of potential service work, how about you take a quick personal inventory to see if you've got what it takes to serve it like a big wet fucking diva, completely soaked to the bone with nasty, gushy fierceness. Are your giant, oily hands peppered with patches of matted hair and thick, impenetrable calluses? Good. Does your glossy forty-eight-inch ponytail detach easily? Are your hooves so riddled with bunions that you can only shop for shoes at the Boot Barn? Got any teeth? Where the fuck is your aunt Trudy? These are all important questions, and while there may not be any important answers, let's go ahead and secure our hairnets anyway. It's time to serve, you fierce fucking bitch!

KATYA: CLEANER

Let's face it: People are really fucking gross. We, as a species, are morally and socially compelled toward an unachievable state of cleanliness that is betrayed by our innately repulsive physiology. As a professional cleaner, you confront the harsh and undeniable evidence of humanity's contempt for itself. Any previous subscription you may have had to a recognizable code of ethics has been long abandoned and replaced by the chaos of unbridled aggression, violence, and endless suffering. The sheets are soaked in blood. The walls are speckled with viscera. The stench of death is a fetid fog that follows you at all times, ubiquitous and unavoidable.

You were once a corporate lawyer who got into some questionable activities on an extended vacation in Mexico City, but now you're a cleaner for the cartels. It all happened so quickly; during brief moments of peace you struggle to recall just how you got yourself mixed up in something so dangerous, so destructive,

so . . . delectable. Ahh, there it is. That's when you remember. It wasn't just your cast-iron stomach and indifference toward dismemberment but your surprising, newly awakened taste for fresh blood and meat.

Suddenly the pieces of the puzzle begin to line themselves up. When the other children would chase the ice cream truck through the neighborhood streets, you would slink away to the woods to rip the skin off rabbits and chew their innards. You didn't just get mixed up with some bad guys or fall into the shadows by mistake. You are and always have been the pure, unadulterated essence of evil. Like a volcanic eruption straight from the bowels of Hell, you were spewed directly out of the mouth of the beast and shot through some innocent woman's uterus, like those tubes they used to have at the bank drive-through. But you are not merely evil; you are evil's nefarious enabler. You remove the carnage of lowly grifters, criminals, and monsters to allow their hideousness to grow and spread into ever more indescribable viciousness.

And while all of that is objectionable, loathsome, and abhorrent, when push comes to shove and some dumb bitch spills her cabernet on my silk rug, you'd be the first person I'd call to save the day. On the off chance you happen to be, like, a regular house cleaner, you'd be the second person I would call, especially considering it's just a matter of time before cleaner number one is tidily disposed of one day.

TRIXIE: SERVER

Serving in a restaurant is the hardest job there is. Go ahead and process that controversial yet brave proclamation . . . I'll wait. The only people who don't think servers have it hard are people who have never been a server themselves. In Los Angeles, there are a shocking number of people who do not tip and who believe that people who have menial positions such as servers have somehow "brought it on themselves." Karma has apparently kissed them because they are deserving of love and light and their waitress should have taken night classes if she didn't want to be a waitress. These are also typically people who have familial wealth and have never worked a job because they needed it. When the servers start poisoning the Coke Zero, these people will go first.

Serving is so much more than bringing food: Knowing the menu, cleaning the tables, rolling silverware, processing payments, having full-on screaming matches with kitchen staff across a language barrier, and crying in the freezer are just a few of the lesser-known duties. The other less-mentioned trauma of this job is that each table has a different definition of what good service is. Some people want to be left alone almost entirely. They want to order, eat, and leave without even hearing your name or remembering you were there. Meanwhile, some people need fellatio, a personal anecdote, and a good cry before they can even think about appetizers. Reading the energy of a group means going full Sybil Dorsett from table to table and is an essential customer service skill.

On top of all that, you are dealing with *food*. Everyone's preferences, diets, and allergies are being thrown into the nightly off-Broadway performance of *Pretending to Care About People: The New Musical*, and you are also expected to roll 350 silverware sets before the dinner rush. This is all done in hopes that the customer remembers that they are solely in control of your salary that day.

When all the customer service world agrees to participate in the Purge, servers will be at the head of the pack: Mad Max–style renegades who have been hardened into cold warriors by lunch specials and singing "Happy Birthday" to strangers. The next time you are seated in a restaurant and you insist on ten separate checks, remember that you could be incurring the wrath of a long-overdue revolution. Every waitress packs her apron with *Braveheart* face paint and a butterfly knife. Your food isn't late; it's done already, dehydrating under a heat lamp. Because you were just a rude bitch.

KATYA: NANNY

There's nothing quite like looking after rich folks' kids. Whether you are a magical Englishwoman who rides an umbrella to work or a mouthy brunette with a love for pattern problems and teased hair, there's no doubt about it—the nanny is where it's at. Can you think of another job where you get to horse around with well-behaved children for a couple hours a day and in return, you get to wear the mom's clothes and have all the sex you want with the dad? You also get to live rent-free in a beautiful nanny nook out back, where all the utilities are fully paid for.

Now, I know what you're thinking: sounds boring. But what if I told you that being a nanny isn't just about sex, money, and giggling? If you're in the market for something a little more dangerous, there's always *The Hand That Rocks the Cradle* school of childcare. This exciting nanny position requires no experience, although it does help if you've been recently pregnant and widowed. All you have to do is choose a fake name, infiltrate the loving home of a beautiful couple, and methodically destroy that home from the inside as the unassuming nanny. You also get to do fun side activities like killing the mom's nosy best friend when she inevitably gets hip to your scheme. If all of the above sounded nice to you but you live abroad, guess what? You could be an au pair, which is basically just a nanny who wears a beret! Ooh la la!

TRIXIE: RETAIL

Time is a beast of absolute meter. An eight-hour shift at any job is eight hours—unless it's a retail shift. In retail, time manspreads on the subway bench of life in a way that defies possibility. Even a three-hour shift at the wrong store in the wrong mall on the wrong day can creep by with impressive restraint. You check the clock after what you are sure has been twelve hours to find that you haven't even made it to your fifteen-minute break. Sure that you are looped in some sort of time-space redundancy, you sprint to Health and Beauty, where you burn your inner thigh with a hot curling iron to reset reality. Time sadly doesn't reset, and you must limp over to the sale gondola and begin refolding the denim. Folding, refolding, and re-refolding are just a few of the dynamic tasks that retail offers.

Retail also offers the unique opportunity to be a conduit of undiluted hate. At least servers are *needed*. I think in most stores, customers wish that the employees didn't exist. They'd rather thumb through used vinyl without you asking, "Looking for anything specific?" to which they must provide a banal "I'm just looking." The phrase "I'm just looking" is Navajo for "Leave me alone, you fucking cunt." Customers don't really ever need help—and if they do, they'll find you and scream at you like a rehomed parakeet. The customer values the part of shopping where they have to find their item. I once heard that at the Buckle, the employees are encouraged to interact with the customer three times before they leave the store. I would rather be hit by a car in the parking lot than be asked to open a store credit card.

TRIXIE: BARTENDER

One thing is for sure: Drunk people are awful. Babbling, volatile adult babies with limp dicks and puke-soaked fishtail braids. The inebriated need service, entertainment, and a ringleader with a questionably "clean" rag, aka a bartender. Bartenders are the *Touched by an Angel* angels of the customer service industry. They are actively selling a product that slowly makes their customers' behavior become unpredictable and obnoxious. Bartenders have to memorize an infinite number of drink recipes just so Beth from the bridal party can get her Hurricane Orgasm Facefucker Panty Pudding Shot the night before the nuptials. Bartenders are also natural-born bouncers when it comes down to it, so don't be surprised when the happy-hour shift lead chucks you into the street for implying that the beer is warm.

And have you ever noticed that the bottles in a bar appear in perfect order? The bartenders have to know where every single bottle belongs *by heart*. I think when a bartender gets to Heaven, Jesus soaks a tampon in SKYY vodka and shoves it right up their hole. In a perfect world, bar staff would board planes first and the gate attendant would say, "Thank you for your service," as "America the Beautiful" played. But we don't live in that world, so apply at your own risk.

KATYA: HOTEL HOUSEKEEPER

Hotel housekeepers are required to provide a spotless environment that will immediately be ransacked with no care or consideration for their efforts, and also to literally never be seen. Sometimes, specifically at resorts and beach vacation spots, they also fold the towels into vacation-related origami. And yet, some people still have the nerve to not tip their housekeeper. If a traveler doesn't have twenty bucks a night to tip their housekeeper, then they shouldn't be staying in a hotel. Many people who travel often aren't paying for their own hotel rooms; they are reimbursed by their employers. The amount of travel they do should give them an even deeper understanding of the level of rigor the housekeeping job takes, and yet they still fumble the bag on the tip.

Reader, do you really think you have the nerve, the skill, the stomach, or the level of up-and-coming ambitious hip-hop-artist hustle required to succeed in this particular industry? I submit that you don't have the cojones to create a sparkling, tranquil, orderly environment so that the unimpressed throng of miserable Pigpens you serve are set up to relax, succeed, or do whatever the hell they do. Let's have a glance at some of the daily obligations attended to on a very short time crunch by the average hotel housekeeper. Take a walk in these well-worn Keds for a look at the horrors that may await you:

- Peel the puke-stained sheets off a king bed and replace them with fresh linens, assembled with surgical precision.

- Suck a petri dish's worth of dust out of crusty Reagan-era carpets using a congested vacuum cleaner.

- Perform biblical-level miracles in the form of removing a variety of stains from various surfaces.

- Clean a bathroom. Period. If you're reading this book, I want you to put it down and look at your bathroom and tell me if it's clean. Would you feel embarrassed if someone famous and important showed up and asked if they could use your bathroom? Yeah, I thought so. I spend a few minutes at least every day wondering how I would feel if I heard suddenly that Sharon Stone is going to come to my door and say, "Hi, I'm Sharon Stone, and I was wondering if I could use your bathroom. It's an emergency." The most likely way that scenario would play out is me spinning a rushed and tangled series of yarns explaining not only why my toilet was nonfunctional but also how three toxic coats of antique paint just rolled onto all four walls around the toilet. Then I would offer a glass of tea and compassionately suggest that while the kettle gets to boiling, I could escort her to the garage out back and keep watch while she pissed in my empty parking spot.

Whether or not you pursue a gig in housekeeping, keep the following points in mind: If a cleaner is going to steal something of yours while in the vicinity of your belongings, let them. I'm gonna let you in on some facts: 99.9 percent of the time when people jump to conclusions and accuse their cleaner or housekeeper of stealing, they're wrong. And the 0.1 percent who allows for the possibility that it actually was stolen, she deserved it, that greedy bitch. And I hope that Linda from housekeeping enjoys that costume jewelry and has an amazing time.

TRIXIE: PERSONAL ASSISTANT

There is one type of job that brings being in the service industry to a whole new level: personal assistant. I'm not saying I abuse my personal assistant, but let's just say that when he watches *The Handmaid's Tale*, he is particularly moved by Offred's courage. Assistants assist, which means whatever your boss is doing, you are now doing.

Assistants do exciting projects like red carpets, planning events, and elaborate trips—but my assistant also folds my laundry, washes makeup brushes, and stocks my fridge with Bubly. Living in Los Angeles has invited to my ears

countless tales of personal assistance gone awry: sex scandals, theatrical firings, and standing outside Glossier for hours to buy Boy Brow.

It's probably ideal to maintain one assistant over a stretch of time, but most clients run through personal assistants like Caitlyn Jenner behind the wheel of a car. Personal assistants can ensure job security by babying their wards to the point of psychological regression. Pretty soon you can't be fired or replaced because you're the only one who knows the Wi-Fi password and the numerical key to the guesthouse.

I know you're itching to get to the sweet office gigs in the next chapter, but not so fast, Dilbert! It must be said. Repeat after me: Tipped laborers are the backbone of society. So before we move on, I present:

A Love Letter to the Tipped Laborer
by Katya

If you choose not to pursue a career in the service industry, I suggest that you make a habit of overtipping. There is nothing that a server could ever do to me that would result in me not leaving a tip. There have been situations where the server has been dismissive, been outwardly rude, brought out the wrong food, and argued about the wrong food they brought out, and I've always tipped. The server could emerge three hours late wearing an oversize Tweety Bird sweatshirt and dump a scalding bowl of bouillabaisse (that I did not order) in my lap, and when he refuses to help me clean myself, I'll be calculating the 20–25 percent tip as he leaves the restaurant to let the air out of my tires. The hotel-housekeeper-tipping rules apply here: If you can't afford a standard tip at a restaurant or bar, you should be at home having Hamburger Helper instead. There is no way to argue against raising guaranteed wages for tipped laborers without looking like an out-of-touch upper-cruster born with a huge silver spoon up your ass. And if the shoe fits, wear it! And then make sure that Nordy's salesgal who brought you the shoes gets her full commission.

When it comes to the gig economy, remember that workers like Uber drivers and Postmates—they aren't exactly doing it because they have a passion for transporting drunk sorority girls and overpriced nachos. Also, always give them a five-star rating. If they kill your family, four stars.

Let me tell you an interesting story about the power of tipped laborers. Late one evening, I ordered cinnamon breadsticks from Domino's, which come with a delicious container of icing that I refer to as "White Diamonds." This icing is *essential* for the enjoyment of the breadsticks, so much so that the infrequent but traumatizing instances when a delivery is made with the nightmarish lack of said icing, it's like driving cross-country with no tires. Or jumping on a bike with the seat missing.

So, the food arrived, and seconds after the driver left, I opened the box, excited to enjoy my little treat, only to discover the icing was not in the box. The degree of emotional devastation cannot be overstated here. I felt like Helen Hunt in *Twister* when the tornado snatched away her father—a traumatic event that sent her on her life course to become a PhD-level meteorologist with a death wish that involved walking into tornadoes. Imagine how people who lost loved ones in the planes on 9/11 felt, then multiply that by twenty. I was left with two choices: commit suicide, or call Domino's and see if they could bring over a container of icing.

After much consideration, I picked up the phone and called them, and they agreed to send over the missing icing. When the delivery boy arrived, he was so apologetic that he would not accept the tip I offered him. He could only focus on his mistake. But I insisted that he take the tip, because what he didn't know is that by correcting his mistake, he prevented me from killing myself. By arriving with not one, but two twin towers of Domino's breadstick icing, he reversed twenty 9/11s of emotional terrorism. Ten bucks was the least I could do. After all, you can't put a price on peace.

This is all to say that tipped laborers work small miracles every day, but all too often their actions are only highlighted if something is wrong, and they're rarely rewarded for doing their job. You'll never be on your deathbed thinking, "Damn, I wish I had tipped the Domino's guy less."

How do I have so much insight into the dynamic between the tipper and tippee, you ask? Well, Sandy, it's quite simple. I, too, have done my time

ramming my fist into the tip jar for extra quarters. Don't forget that these are the humble beginnings of most drag queens, at least before they started *ka-ka-ka-kowing* out of the womb ready to be Top 4 on *Drag Race* and go to the Met Gala.

Picture this: It's a Wednesday night, mid-July of 2012. Two showgirls and I are applying the finishing touches to our makeup as we prepare for another riveting night of lip-syncing to absolutely no one. It's a strange feeling to do a show for zero people in the audience, and even stranger to do it for ninety minutes. You start to wonder if you're living in some kind of David Lynch movie—and at the end of the night, when you slink out of there penniless, it starts to feel more like a Clint Eastwood film, *Zero Dollar Baby*.

But that night, ten minutes into the show, a miracle occurred. A mirage of sexy WAGs* materialized out of the humid summer air; a dozen or so young ladies (who we would later find out were the romantic and sexual partners of the New England Patriots) had come to deliver us from our plight in a dazzling display of strip club generosity usually reserved for the rapper's elite.

It was pure magic: They came in and threw wads and wads of dollar bills at us, so much that we had to sweep them off the stage with a broom! We didn't even have a broom, but there we were, sweeping that cash off the stage and into our suitcases. I wish we could say that we deserved it, but we didn't. Does an uncoordinated series of pelvic gyrations punctuated by halfhearted hairography necessarily call for seven hundred dollars in tips? Of course not, but this is America.

When the bar's ATM was sucked dry halfway through the show, one of the ladies gleefully went on a cash run, determined to see the night's decadent festivities flare to the very end. The coup de grâce: A petite but very intense woman in seven-inch cork espadrilles mounted the stage in a fury of drunken determination, came toward me with a fistful of dollar bills, and hurled it right at my face. They say that you can't just throw money at a problem to fix it? Well, this time it worked. Thank you, Rich Football Lady, for paying this struggling gay person's August rent.

* Women and girlfriends of professional athletes

I wish this fate on every girl who's out there working for tips. You, too, should experience a *The Shining*–style flooding, but instead of blood, it's sexy sports wives armed with hundreds and hundreds of dollar bills. May they infiltrate drag bars, valet parking lots, massage parlors, and babysitters clubs across the nation, pockets bursting with bills, and make it rain on each of you. When you're a tipped worker, your fate rests in the hands of the eternally dissatisfied consumer. On these rare occasions, you experience a miraculous intervention in the manicured hands of a WAG who is willing to look past your dazzlingly mediocre display of "talent" and reward you like you're Rihanna. It's the Domino's icing on the cake.

WHAT KIND OF JOB DO YOU WANT?

BY KATYA

Office Work Edition

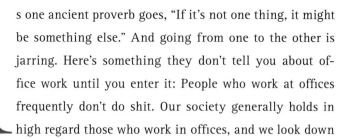

As one ancient proverb goes, "If it's not one thing, it might be something else." And going from one to the other is jarring. Here's something they don't tell you about office work until you enter it: People who work at offices frequently don't do shit. Our society generally holds in high regard those who work in offices, and we look down on customer service professionals, which would make you think that the office is some well-oiled machine. In reality, it's an iPod Nano that won't turn on anymore that you found at the bottom of your old backpack. It's all a charade—productivity theater, if you will. All the world's a stage, so grab your wig and make sure you know your lines.

At the Orange Julius, you were putting on your strict corporate-friendly uniform and getting worked like a marine for eight hours with one state-sanctioned unpaid break. Now, at Acme Corp., you can choose your own outfits, regularly show up late and leave early after putting in sixish hours of loafing at your desk, and take a two-hour business lunch that is not only on the clock, but expensed on your corporate Amex. You also get healthcare and a computer. Some offices even let people bring their dogs, have catered happy hours, and give you money to join a gym. Is this just some bizarre money-laundering scheme? Don't bother to take out your tinfoil hat—it doesn't go great with your outfit.

So, smile and nod, and take in your new office life. And don't forget about the little guys back at the Orange Julius.

Here's a brief overview of some of the fields whose work generally occurs at an office.

PUBLISHING

Well, these are the people who will be assembling this book for its release and could, realistically, put whatever they want in it to make us look bad and we would never know until we're trending on Twitter with the hashtag

#TrixieAndKatyaAreOverParty. Unrelated, but they are all beautiful geniuses whose work is criminally undervalued. I imagine that these offices play lots of relaxing music and everyone dresses in a cozy beige rainbow of brushed linens. I was recently made aware of the Mariko Aoki phenomenon, which is a term for the urge to poop at the bookstore, named after the woman who brought the subject to light in a letter to a Japanese literary magazine. While there is still no definitive answer for why people like to poop at the bookstore, I think it's because we feel like we're at home. Home is where the books are. I would feel so at home at a publishing company's office that I would annihilate their plumbing system.

BIG TECH

A freak show shrouded in indecipherable codes and cloaked in approachable avant-basic day wear. Prepare for HR meetings in VR, adaptogenic beer on tap, and swaths of former high school nerds taking their revenge by doing cosplay of what they think a cool person is. From the outside, it seems like Big Tech offices live every day like Macaulay Culkin when he wakes up and realizes he's home alone. (Wow. I just got the title. Brilliant!) Every day at Tech Company XYZ, they're testing the limits for how much boyish fun can be had in a day—all backed by unimaginable amounts of capital. But all parties must come to an end eventually, and then they have to toss out all the evidence of their hedonism before the family gets back from Paris. Likewise, Big Tech is going to enter its flop era soon, and all Mark Zuckerberg will have going for him is that fat techie dumper.

FINANCE

The halcyon days of *Wall Street* are behind us. If this book was coming out in 1983, my one-year-old self would be sagely telling you to gel your hair back, buy a couple crisp suits, and bring your boss a bottle of quaaludes as a welcome gift, and you'd be golden. But in the Wild, Wild West of cryptocurrency (which has nothing to do with crypts, unfortunately), NFTs, and teenagers on the internet manipulating the stock market, the finance sector is no longer a straight (if ho-moerotic) shot.

ENTERTAINMENT AGENCIES

ACTION! CUT! SOUND SPEEDING! SOFT STICKS! Ah, the sounds of Hollywood. But you don't need to be a starving artist who's gotta sleep your way to the top to make it big. You can be that floozy's agent! Entertainment agencies are full of dreamy-eyed hotshots who showed up to LA with twenty-five dollars and a degree from NYU and want to be the next Mr. Joanne Netflix. Despite most movies nowadays being glorified commercials with dialogue written by an algorithm, there is still an army of agency employees who send emails twenty-four hours a day. You might hear an agency assistant describe their job as "covering a desk." Let me be the first to tell you this does not mean they make tablecloths. You only make that mistake once!

INSURANCE

This sector is great for those of you who can't wait to work for the devil but still have some time left here on Earth before your eternity in Hell. This grim nine-to-five combines the thrill of gambling with the morbidity of contract killing, but all from the comfort of a poorly lit, major-depression-inducing office environment. Playing the slots can get old, but you know what doesn't get old? Deb in Des Moines, who just kicked the bucket because she couldn't afford life-saving treatment because it was not covered by your company. But listen, don't feel sad; there's no time for that. You've got a ton of sick people waiting on hold who don't know their coverage stopped a month ago, and they're just itching to get the news. But if the guilt does somehow manage to seep in, you always have the option of simply not doing your job, as evidenced by the lovely worker with whom I spent two hours on the phone—and, when I followed up, had absolutely no record of me ever calling. How fun!

OFFICE ATTIRE

You Want to Make Money?

Wear a Suit

BY TRIXIE

Whether or not you believe in corporations, money, capitalism, or any other systems that are so casually thrown around in this book, you must be at a place in your life where you believe in dressing for the job you want. You bought this book, for example: a workplace manual written by a flighty drug addict and an emotionally stunted fag who skips close family funerals for self-appointed workplace commitments. Point being, you didn't buy this book because we are smart, successful, or even technically employed in the eyes of the IRS. You bought this book because we are a couple of snake-oil charlatans who tricked you into believing we are authors

whose word paths deserve traversing. You have been lied to, yes, but Barnes & Noble is in the suburbs and you don't plan on going back until Thanksgiving, when you usually fight with your bitch of a mom at dinner, so there's no returning it now. The snare was set, and you walked into it like a glossy-eyed fawn. No refunds.

But how did we do it? Simply put, we dressed for the job. What is drag if not a by-the-book expression of dressing for success? You grab a wig, some fabric, and two lashes, you dress like society's idea of a young, beautiful, and rich person, and *poof!* Literary goddesses, party of two! Dean Koontz and Janet Evanovich reporting to shake down the bisexual middle schoolers for their daddy's money. Again, we aren't celebrities, but we play them on TV. We are two bald fags with few discernible gifts who stumbled into an "art" form that allows us to masquerade as humans worthy of life and love. Ergo, the power of dressing for success.

DRESS FOR THE JOB YOU WANT? OR DRESS FOR THE JOB YOU HAVE?

Dressing for the job you want has to be balanced with dressing for the job you are actually currently occupying. Perhaps you are a young girl who has skated her entire life, with only one more Olympic qualifying year in you. Perhaps nature has cruelly turned against you with the maturation of your heavy naturals, which offset your center of gravity. Does that mean you should be working the morning window shift at Starbucks in a sequin skate costume and bisecting lines of heavy cream blush? You know, in writing this section I meant to paint a discouraging example, but if the employees at Starbucks looked triple-axel-ready, I might drink more coffee.

Like the f-word or anything versatile and effective, it's important to not abuse the tools. Getting a clean fade before your quarterly review is a nice touch. Maybe even a spritz of cologne before the office holiday party just to add some depth to your shallow character of "the Temp." However, going full tailcoat tuxedo because you heard your superior is going on maternity leave is an example of too much of a good thing. Restraint is key here. A little jewelry or a fresh pair of stockings can communicate "management material" better than looping the office floor with a "World's Best Boss" mug in tow. Remember to edit. Think of it this way: If there was an actual World's Best Boss award, it probably wouldn't be a dime-store tchotchke made to hold instant coffee. It would probably be early retirement.

DOUBLE STANDARDS IN OFFICE ATTIRE

It's impossible to muse on work attire without acknowledging the obvious double standards surrounding the subject. Gender, rank, and race are just a few of the perennial pitfalls that plague the workplace. Why does the mailroom clerk at Facebook have to wear loafers to be taken seriously while Mark Zuckerberg gets to dress like he works at Old Navy? Why are Black employees discouraged from dressing like anything but a cartoon of a boring suburban Caucasian just to make it through the first interview? Why do women have to basically present *Project Runway* during office hours, while men in general serve chinos and a golf shirt that has truthfully never seen sunlight, let alone a driving range? These questions and answers are circular in that they all revolve around broken systems that we are forced to participate in *just by getting a job*. The rancid broth of these broken systems cannot be distilled by two cross-dressers in a satirical coffee table book such as the one you're reading, but we can at least mention it before we shit all over it.

Women who wear a full beat for work are the true whores of modern society. Call me broken, call me dark-sided, but I love nothing more than walking into an establishment and being greeted by a lacquered-up hourly employee. LAX used to have Delta flights leaving from Terminal 6, and there was a Russian woman who worked at TSA in Delta SkyPriority. I usually would end up on the first flight out for a gig because you lose hours traveling from Los Angeles. Even at 5:30 a.m., when I would pass through security, barely functional and hungover, I was regularly humbled by the presence of this painted-up prostitute. Slicked-back bleached-blond hair, blue smoky eye, lashes, red-lacquered lip, and contour that even gave me, Tina Marino, a run for my money. Whenever I am awake at 4:00 a.m. heading to the airport, I can't help but imagine Miss Russia getting fully stamped for the gig and showing up looking like she is leaving work to do straight porn. I saw myself in her, and I still relate to her to this day.

UNIFORMS

If you have to wear a uniform, here are some tips to spice it up:

- You're in the army? Add some rhinestones or sequins to your uniform before heading out to the battlefield so you stand out.

- If you have to work in fast food, why not look like a fast girl? Remove your polyblend polo. Wear the visor as a confusing but revealing tube top. Pumps can be slippery on greasy tile, but falling is a great way to communicate vulnerability and relatability to potential mates in the vicinity.

- If you're a flight attendant, it really depends on which airline you're a part of. If you're on Virgin Australia, you're pretty much ready to slay. Chic chignon, flattering neck scarf, and a face full of Sherwin-Williams interior semigloss? Work, bitch. Are you with Emirates? A timeless red lip and an iconic piece of headwear. I live. However, if you are with United or Aer Lingus, you really have no hope. Liberal amounts of perfume might be the only way to elevate the look to sea level.

EDUCATION

The
Library
Is Open

BY TRIXIE

In a truly shocking turn of events that no one ever saw coming, Katya and I are both college educated. Granted, I went to a state school for musical theater, which is the Golden Corral of idiots who won't stop singing and sadly will hit a career peak dancing on TikTok. And Katya went to some freaky-deeky choose-your-own-adventure arts program in Massachusetts. (I'd not put my faith in my education in the hands of a state that was burning witches relatively recently.)

But I guess you could say that we are two rare cases that use our college educations on a regular basis. We might be circus monkeys for bachelorettes, but our minds have been fed and watered by the educational system enough to be full-size monkey brains. We think about bananas, peanuts, *and* the theory of relativity. Specifically, I think about how much writing I have left in this chapter relative to the amount of writing I have left in the book as a whole.

Before we dive in, let me stress that you don't need education to work. But there are types of jobs that will be easier to excel at with certain types of education. Some places will require a formal paper saying you jumped through academic hoops. Some jobs won't require any training but you will find yourself activated like a sleeper soldier with developed skills from your schooling. Whatever happens, it's likely you'll need a job to pay back your student loans or put yourself through school, so whatever way you wade the waters of employment, I want you to be an A+ student *and* an A+ employee.

HIGH SCHOOL

High school is something that I don't think you can really avoid. You could be homeschooled, but usually that comes attached to an oppressive religious practice or having really old parents. You may not realize it, but if you have a chalkboard in your dining room that your father uses to teach you physics, there is a 100 percent chance you are wearing a floor-length linen skirt and people assume your elderly mother is your grandma. You love showing cats at 4-H, you are a virtuosic pianist, and you can't wait to go on a mission trip with your cousin Jebediah. You might not even be offended by this assessment as you have already decided that I am going to Hell™ and you are going to pray for me. Amen, sister. See you at brunch.

While the perpetual snow day of homeschooling is appealing, it's much more likely that you will receive a standard high school education. Or not receive it so much as be present in the room while adults talk at you for four years. Hollywood seems to glamorize high school in films and television and to oversell the experience as some sort of formative chrysalis from which you are intended to emerge fully formed. *Grease, High School Musical, Clueless*—all parables of development and coming of age in which the protagonists are basically fairy-tale versions of teens played by thirty-year-olds. (Stockard Channing was thirty-three when she played Rizzo in *Grease*. This shocking age differential inspired the plot of the movie *The Orphan*.)

It is communicated to us at a young age that our high school experiences are to be fraught with sex, heightened dialogue, and bouncy ponytails. This is where our tongues-speaking homeschooled neighbors have it figured out, because they are missing out on nothing. The same way Santa was invented by department stores to upsell gift-wrapping services, high school was invented by the office supply industry to sell number two pencils. The homeschooled receive an actual education while we the cattle get peer-pressured into Sadie Hawkins dances. Across the globe, Mr. Dixon Ticonderoga buys an island in the Palisades and the cycle continues.

Of course, there are differences between public and private high school experiences, but from what I have learned dating a man who grew up rich (Wicker Park rich, not oil tycoon in Dubai rich), the experiences are mostly parallel. Instead of someone's dad being a violent alcoholic who messes his pants, someone's mom is constipated on prescription painkillers and hasn't pooped in weeks. Instead of being embarrassed because your father is wearing pajama pants to pick you up from school, you are embarrassed because your mother, Charlize Theron, keeps getting catcalled at PTA meetings. While it would be nice to emerge from graduation like Julia Stiles in *10 Things I Hate About You*, confidently sweetened by the experience, it's much more likely you'll be channeling one Sidney Prescott from Woodsboro High. Blood spattered, crying, and having outlived all your friends by a thin eleventh-hour spark of bravery, you live to be pursued by Death another day: your first semester in college.

COLLEGE ADMISSIONS

So you've decided to pursue postsecondary education. (Or does college count as secondary education? Tertiary? I don't know. There's probably an associate's degree for this type of knowledge.) You put up your hair in two neat braids and you've had your morning coffee. You've selected your most capable-looking outfit from Fred Segal. You're ready to conquer the academic world and push play on the sequel to high school: COLLEGE. Not so fast! After high school, participating in education becomes a selective process. You need to be either a good person, a smart person, or an athletic person. Sadly, it also helps to have a

Caucasian-sounding name, but we can't dive into the inherent racism of the admissions process just now. Admissions is basically the bald guy outside the club deciding who gets to cut the line based on their social stature or their look. You'd better be Cindy Crawford's daughter or dressed like a club kid or you're going to have to freeze outside with the plebians.

For some of you little goody-goodies reading this book, this admissions section will seem like a firm, encouraging pat on the bottom. You already have the impressive report card. You already rescue ducklings covered in oil in your spare time. You even spend your weekends counseling the sexually assaulted using puppets and an acoustic guitar. Breezing into your college of choice will be as easy as using a Waterpik, and your future is a swinging saloon door of opportunities. You'll be able to use the proper channels to further your education and you should either skip to the "Master's and Beyond" section of this chapter, or read no further.

Now I'd like to address the goons and goblins at the back of the classroom. The lazy, the stupid, and the other never-meant-to-be folks among us. Of course you'd love to attend your college of choice, but even researching this dream college took the wind out of your sails and left you breathless and exhausted. Your grades are in the gutter, you actually *eat* oiled ducklings, and the most selfless thing you've ever done is not fart in your girlfriend's Subaru.

Get ready to scheme your way to the middle by putting into action my absolving admissions cover letter. All you have to do is add a few first names here and fudge a couple factoids and you're practically headed for an early graduation. Buckle up, though, because for some of you nimrods, this might be the closest thing to homework you've ever done.

Dear _____ (Yale, Harvard, Hogwarts),

My name is _____ (if you haven't figured out how to fill this space, I can't help you) and I'm so happy to be seeking admission to your school. I was eating a hot Cup O' Noodles in my Mazda when an ad came on the radio that you were selling diplomas for about _____ per semester and I immediately pulled over. My mother always said that opportunity knocks but once—and she would know. She was murdered by a tumor that she ignored in her forties. She's fine now; honestly, when it comes to adversarial marriages, sometimes dead is better.

As a senior at _____ (Rydell High, Torrance High, Sunnydale High) I have a wealth of experience in _____, _____, and covering up a student-teacher romance. Sure, the sneaking around made it hotter, but the real risk involved was the other teachers finding out and getting jealous. Picture it: my full breasts bobbing in the teachers' lounge restroom as Vice Principal McClarkson microwaves his lunch for an additional thirty seconds. Little did he know that his lunch would soon be procured by me after climax and I would later eat the hot Cup O' Noodles in my Mazda.

Some of my relevant high school experiences include:

- Freelance cheerleading. We didn't have a squad per se, but I love yelling and jumping.

- Fly-fishing. My team, "Pretty Fly for a Walleye," went to nationals twice. We actually invented the eyebrow piercing during a local Fish-O-Rama after some careless casting. After the stitches came out, every punk band in the state was rocking a brow ring!

- Debate. I was actually the one who pushed for companion animals on Delta domestic flights. I wasn't emotionally unstable; I just wanted celebrities in Los Angeles to be able to fly with ill-behaved rats in tow and Instagram about it.

I've enclosed my résumé, which may or may not be a copy-paste job from Hilary Swank's IMDb. Essentially, the information is the same. We both are strong women with a flair for dramatic acting and a willingness to do whatever it takes to work with Clint Eastwood at some point. Please have your people contact my people and we can do what we were meant to do: dRoP tHe CoLlAb SiS.

Love, _____

COLLEGE

College ends up being the experience you wanted your time in high school to be. College makes high school seem like a pubescent waiting room where everyone has acne and no one has access to booze. After leaving high school, your skin clears up, you discover alcohol, and your social life is truly born of your new freedom. You can skip class, which regretfully I never did. Not necessarily because I didn't want to but because I paid for this full education and my Native American grandmother taught me to use the whole animal. I am also too much of a goody-goody when push comes to shove, and breaking rules has always frightened me. The fear of failure and pursuit of perfection I exhibited in college have calcified inside me and created an adult who is truly horrible to work for. Tardiness, disengagement, flakiness: all fireable offenses with no warning at Trixie Mattel LLC.

You can have lots of sexual experiences, roommate permitting. It's tough when everyone around you is at a sexual peak but no one has any privacy. I once did anal with two men in the bottom bunk of my dorm room while my roommate slept on the top bunk. I was convinced at that moment that he was a deep sleeper and that we just had to be quiet. Looking back, we were not quiet, and he was fully awake the entire time. I also at eighteen had not discovered douching or lube, so by the time my roommate woke up, let's just say there was more than one irritated asshole in the room.

College is also a great opportunity to find like-minded individuals and double down on personality traits and interests that you had previously considered unappealing. Making friends is extremely easy: that Digimon card collection you are still working on that you started when you were nine? Well, guess what, Mary, there's a Digimon orgy in the quad at noon that is benefiting the on-campus Trans Wellness Center. Do you believe that life is precious and starts at conception? Meet up with the gals outside the student union to paint Cabbage Patch dolls with fake blood and throw them at the liberal arts majors. Are you

literally a disgusting, rip-roaring racist? Sadly, there's probably an intramural softball team of dumb white people starting up in the spring.

At the risk of sounding at all optimistic, college is conversely an opportunity to become more yourself by bouncing off other walks of life. Speaking from personal experience, I always knew I was a little gay. But being in theater school gave me an environment to crystallize into the gay icon you see today. Everyone around me was gay and no one cared, and I became like a koi fish of gayness, expanding to the size of my gay container, which was suddenly the gay ocean. I tap-danced, sucked cock, and cross-dressed all the way to graduation, which I ultimately didn't attend because I didn't have forty dollars for the cap and gown. (Being gay didn't become lucrative until a few years later.) In my case, a performing arts degree directly aided my success as a performance artist. However, if you end up with a master's in sociology and you end up a lovely valet, don't say I didn't warn you.

TRADE SCHOOL

Don't get too excited, you gay, gay fag. While hot pieces of trade might be attending trade school, that's not what the term means. Trade school is basically any type of vocational school where you intensely learn about your new career. You learn the complete handbook in a shorter period of time than university and you leave with a skill that you can use to actually make money. Imagine! After a four-year college program, you leave with debt, confusion, some gained weight, and a rolled-up piece of paper that you aren't even clear on how to frame and mount. While a university education guarantees nothing, trade school spits you out on your feet with the means to start cashing checks. Your first job? Hanging a communications-degree diploma for some idiot who just finished college.

Pricing can vary—I went to beauty school at the Aveda Institute of Beauty and Wellness in Milwaukee, which was twenty thousand dollars. For cosmetology! Twenty K for learning to trim bangs and give perms. That's like a year of private school. The kicker is I didn't even get to finish beauty school because I was cast in *RuPaul's Drag Race* in the middle of my program and basically had to skip town in the night and not tell anyone. Twenty K down the tube. I'll never financially recover.

MASTER'S AND BEYOND

What comes after undergraduate degrees is a white noise of people who are either overachievers here to make us all look stupid or mentally unwell people who need the routine of schooling to stay pinned together. In most cases, a master's is just a prolonged adolescence with a side of being deceived into believing people care about how someone else's 450-word short story made you feel.

Law school, for example, is a smattering of the smartest kids from every town being grouped together by a blinding desire to argue. Imagine these four-eyed bitches assembling every day to turn a basic traffic-stop scenario into a complete *Roe v. Wade* situation. My brother, an attorney who runs his own practice, is the LeBron James of our family. Dan is the most educated, the most impressive, and even the tallest. He said that law school is extremely challenging. While it is only three years, it's three years after you just finished your four-year undergraduate degree. He said it's nonstop studying, and finals are composed of complicated scenarios where you are expected to apply the semester's teachings on paper and have it evaluated. He also told me he's never seen *Legally Blonde*, so it's hard to take his education seriously at this point.

Med school? This could be just speculation, but I think it would be an interesting mix of people obsessed with the children's board game Operation and people learning to shoot up their own heroin. One of my friends who has a PhD does bodybuilding competitions and may or may not employ the use of steroids. At least he's injecting with a foundation of physiological knowledge, which is more than I can say for drag queens in Orlando. For most PhD students, bodybuilding sadly won't be the chosen path. Most PhD students triumphantly finish a decade of schooling only to return to those hallowed halls as the teachers. Best-case scenario, the graduate goes on to become a real medical professional. Ugly scrubs and an expectation to touch the ill? Yikes, bitch. However, I believe medical professionals are encouraged to wear Crocs, which must be nice.

When the alumni center starts calling you for donations, truly laugh them off the phone.

INTERVIEW WITH A VAMPIRE

BY KATYA

R ight off the bat, I must admit that I do not have a ton of personal experience in this matter. The only formal job interview that I have attended was in a group setting for a pyramid scheme to sell kitchen knives (see "Scams" chapter), and at the end of it, I was told by the leader that I definitely did not possess the necessary qualities or personality traits required for success in the door-to-door knife-slinging business. I left the group interview and pitifully wept in the car as I drove away, only to be pulled over by a state trooper who then yelled at me for driving too slow on the highway. I loudly sobbed as I raced at ninety-five miles an hour the rest of the way home.

My brief and unconventional experience of the interview process may not be at all relatable, helpful, or illuminating to you in any way, so allow me to describe it in detail. My longest-running job was at a family-run shop on the East Coast that sold costumes, wigs, shoes, jewelry, and anything else that wasn't nailed down. It was an eclectic emporium where the fringes of the Northeast would mix and mingle to often hilarious effect.

I was in the store shopping for some drag clothes when I met the owner, Giovanni, who was replacing a watch battery for an old Russian man while an exotic dancer in the market for some new gear was enjoying a little heroin nap on the floor in her seven-inch chrome heels. When I asked if they were hiring, Giovanni looked up, and as he smiled I caught a glimpse of a large front tooth in a haunting shade of antique bone gray and he said, "You never know." He grabbed a piece of cardboard from the trash and handed it to me. I printed my name and number, handed it back, and left.

About a week later, I got a call from Giovanni at the store. He appeared to be in the middle of loudly and publicly firing someone when he asked if I could come in and start work in five minutes but preferably sooner like right now would be preferable. In a couple of years I was managing the store and was handed the burden of having to interview prospective employees, which, like every other thing on my to-do list, I deeply loathed and fiercely dreaded.

I was quickly able to identify some pretty significant red flags—traits or behaviors that you should avoid at all costs, at least during the interview process. For example, try as hard as you possibly can to avoid doing heroin before you sit down with a potential employer. I had a girl nod off mid-sentence as she was describing her leadership qualities. This was concerning, to say the least. But when she snapped right back to life and continued the thought exactly where she'd left off, I was so impressed, I hired her on the spot without bothering to check any of her references—partly because she didn't list any but mostly because we just needed the help during Halloween. There was one guy who came in for his interview in a velvet cloak and large dark sunglasses and would only communicate in a low whisper. That was a nonstarter, though we dated on and off for two years. Then there was the weird Scottish girl who came in singing, drunk as a skunk, but with so much conviction and brawny confident swagger that she refused to fill out an application and instead demanded to know when she would be put on the schedule. This kind of thing rarely works, but this store was a magnet for the rare and unworkable. She stayed on for years, and I'll never forget the moment when I told her I was gay and she asked me how my Nat King was feeling. "Nat King?" I looked at her, puzzled. "Aye, Nat King. Nat King Cole, rhymes with hole." I guess she just assumed I must have done anal earlier that day and was courteous enough to inquire about the state of my asshole.

Anyway, I do have plenty of experience when it comes to the presentation and sale of my body, whether through a TV/film audition or hitting the ho stroll, as it were. When it comes down to it, interviewing for any job is about selling yourself. Except instead of selling yourself as a TV/film character or a sexual partner, you are selling yourself as a responsible, dependable employee who can show up on time, do what is asked of you, and not set anything on fire.

Almost every interview begins with the same core question: First things first, who the hell are you? Do you have any skills? What marketable traits do you possess? You need to really dig deep, ask around, do some research, flip through those baby books, and compile an outrageously thorough inventory of all your assets, talents, achievements, and qualities. This is the perfect time to think about tangible skills like Photoshop, calculus, and accounting, but don't forget about more abstract talents, like interpersonal skills, zodiac sign, and a knack for organization.

Now, some of you might have to face some hard truths, such as: a complete lack of achievements, no discernible talent, and a shocking realization that you are actually quite ugly. Don't worry about it: The focus of this inventory is to identify the assets and discard the liabilities, so if you ain't got shit going on, then we're just starting at the ground floor and there's nowhere to go but up.

At this point, you've probably submitted a résumé and there is at least some level of interest from the employer if they invited you in for an interview. You've gotten a bite on your hook, so it's time to reel them in. But don't get too cocky yet. You need to walk into this experience with the mind of a five-star general, the body of a rhythmic gymnast, the charisma of a mall kiosk cell phone salesman who moonlights as a serial killer, the hands of a Renaissance sculptor, the voice of a fourteenth-century Italian eunuch, the breasts of a Botticelli, the crotch of a Caravaggio, and the swagger of a drunk Russian teen in a TikTok house.

For many people, the job interview experience is fraught with so much fear and anxiety that the nervous system simply shuts down in the same way it would when attacked by a large bear or whale. But, as Kim Cattrall famously said in *Sex and the City 2*, "We have nothing to fear but fear itself," and she was a gorgeous slut who fucked, like, tons of people.

The first thing you need to do is breathe. Take a deep breath in and then hold it for as long as you can, maybe like ten minutes? And then exhale with a loud sigh, and repeat this until you start to feel very dizzy. Once this is complete, find a private space with a mirror. Take a long, hard look at yourself. Note every detail: your pores, the arches of your brows, the priceless gemstone glued to your forehead. Tell yourself that you are a flawless ethereal being who is more powerful than God. Then locate the nearest hammer and shatter the mirror.

Now, let's talk interview attire. Each institution will have its own kind of dress code, so I suggest doing some old-fashioned reconnaissance work to get the clearest picture of your future workplace. A jumpsuit, a bucket of water, a rope, and a fake mustache are easily acquired and the perfect disguise to discreetly survey the sartorial scene. If all else fails, you already have what you need to start a promising career as a window washer.

Office attire and professional wear are often prohibitively expensive and very stressful and depressing to shop for. I worked at a bank for three summers, and I had to wear a button-down shirt and a tie. It was humiliating. I am so grateful to now have a job that allows me to present myself in a way that is much more comfortable, dignified, and true to myself: as an aging Slavic whore.

I've compiled a list of essential items that will help you fearlessly navigate your job interview and secure the job with grace and aplomb.

Interview Day Checklist

☐ References. These can be tough, but everyone seems to love me, so here's my home phone (childhood landline—keeping it REAL): 508-485-4831.

☐ DVD of *Grace and Frankie* or printed out lyrics to "Amazing Grace."

☐ A plum.

☐ A comb just in case you need to flip the script on your hair story.

☐ Business cards—any business cards will do. You can grab a fistful from the deli downstairs or nearest Chinese takeout restaurant. Any business is good business.

☐ Diapers, tampons, and a wool blanket (for electrical fires—ooh, miss thing, you are burning *up*!).

☐ A cast-iron tea set, and plenty (and I mean PLENTY) of loose-leaf tea.

☐ A dossier with the up-to-the-minute whereabouts of the CEO's children, where they go to school, etc. This is especially helpful if the interview goes south and you need to pull a little blackmaily stunt. You can say, "Well, thank you so much for your time. Whatever decision you make, I'm sure it won't affect little Catherine or her tuition at St. Mark's on Fifty-Third Street. I know Mrs. Miller would be worried sick if she didn't show up to Language Arts at eight thirty on a Tuesday," and then give 'em the long stare, wink, stare, smile. Shake hands and press hard.

☐ Vitamins!

☐ Last but not least—and this isn't something you can physically pack— be sure to leave plenty of room for your confidence.

For those of you who are brand-new to this whole thing, have never seen a movie, and have no idea what a job even is, I'll provide you with a sample of a typical interview to give you a sense of the flow of conversation. Let's pretend you are interviewing for an assistant manager position at a store in the mall that sells clocks and whistles. You walk in and meet Wendy, the manager, and sit down in her office.

Wendy: Hello, I am Wendy. Thank you for coming in; I'm excited to get to know you and see if you've got what it takes to hawk these clocks and sling some whistles.

You: It's my pleasure, Wendy, and it just so happens that my passion for time and my lust for blowing are only exceeded by my enthusiasm for sales.

Wendy: That's great to hear. Do you speak Japanese?

You: Yes.

Wendy: Interesting. Are you willing to work nights and weekends?

You: No.

Wendy: Very interesting.

You: Just kidding.

Wendy: HAHAHAHAHAHAHA

You: HAHAHAHAHAHAHA

Wendy: How soon can you start?

See? That was easy. But this scenario is not the norm outside the mall. Most interviews only last about twelve minutes and most decisions are made within the first ten seconds, so let's focus on making the ultimate first impression.

In most professional environments in the West, the handshake is the litmus test for a person's character and ability. I've been a lifelong sufferer of very clammy hands, and since I'm also prone to bouts of anxiety, my handshake can often feel like a wet skeleton hand right out of the microwave, and this puts me at an immediate disadvantage. There is a fun, bold alternative, though: When the other person extends their hand to shake yours, make your hand into a tight fist, and when they grab the stump of your balled-up fingers, it creates a moment of unpredictable curiosity and sets you apart from other applicants.

It's important to maintain perfect posture and sustain eye contact throughout the entire interview but not so much that you appear rigid, haughty, or stiff. A graceful pratfall off the chair with a lighthearted "WHOOPS!" and a quick chuckle as you get up from the floor is a wonderful way to demonstrate your ease and affability.

Another feature that can set you apart as a leading candidate is your smile. Luckily, I am an expert in this subject. If you don't happen to have a mouth full of straight, white teeth, which is often unattainable because dental care is a privilege in this country, fear not! We can work with what we have. Your smile should communicate warmth, sanity, and a healthy sense of humor—often a soft closed-mouth smile will do the trick! Practice for your friends and loved ones until they confirm that you don't look like you electrocute stray dogs in your spare time.

Now that the hard part is over and you are in the door, it's time to sit down and gracefully navigate the even harder part, which is the actual interview. Here are some sample questions and answers that will prepare you for the big day.

Can you tell me a little about yourself?

- *I am a highly motivated person who is willing to do whatever it takes to achieve the highest degree of success in all aspects of my life.*

This answer communicates everything the interviewer wants to know. You're a hustler, and you will bring that same hustle to the job, should you be hired. It's also direct and no-bullshit. Nobody cares that you have a cat, or you love cycling, or you're from Iowa. That doesn't have anything to do with the open project manager role you submitted your application for.

What is your biggest weakness?

- *I can only hold my breath underwater for two minutes.*

This question is a trap for the employer to spot any red flags in your personality. Are you an egomaniac who can't acknowledge your own imperfections? Are you a self-saboteur who will need constant reassurance of your satisfactory performance? One of the well-known taboo answers for this question is "I'm a perfectionist" because it seems like you're trying to show off instead of being vulnerable. It's a cop-out, and nobody wants the police sniffing around their office. That's why I suggest taking the unconventional route instead of succumbing to the pitfalls of the Interview Industrial Complex.

Where do you see yourself in five years?

- *In your chair, wearing your clothes, and asking these very questions.*

Succinct, smooth, and classy as hell. Let them know that you see yourself with the company long-term, and you also admire the interviewer's personal style. It also feels vaguely sexual, which is always a fun energy to bring into the professional environment.

Tell me about a time when you resolved a conflict at work.

- *I acted as a human shield during a violent lunchtime conflict. I absorbed the stab wound very well and was promoted when I returned from medical leave, two weeks early.*

An interview is a great way to tell one memorable story that will stick with them long after you've left. A vivid anecdote punctuated with strong imagery is much more impactful than even the most impressive résumé. It will be hard for the interviewer to remember that you were top of your class at Harvard Business School when the other person has a hilarious story about running into Diane Keaton at the airport and her almost running off with their luggage because they both have the same duffel. This answer is exactly that level of iconic. As a bonus, this particular answer shows how committed and strong you are, and also your ability to quickly heal from physical injury.

How would your coworkers describe you in three words?

- *Borderline personality disorder*

No notes!

Once you're out the door, it's time to take a deep breath and celebrate! But before you get totally blotto, it's always a nice touch to arrange a large basket of fruit and vegetables to be sent to the office of the interviewer with a card that reads only, "Ball's in your court, babe. See you Monday."

THRIVI

PART TWO

NG AT

WORK

TYPES OF COWORKERS

A Field Guide

BY TRIXIE **&** KATYA

KATYA: As the French expression goes, Hell is other people. And the fiery furnace of your place of employment is populated with as many types of demons as Dante's. While in high school and college you could easily avoid any undesirable individuals by means of cliques and specialized extracurriculars, these juvenile systems of exclusion are null in the office. You're gonna have to step up your game. Navigating the bureaucratic bullshit of the average corporate environment takes skill, especially as you encounter and communicate with these boilerplate personalities.

TRIXIE: An office culture by nature relies on the petri dish being full of germs, viruses, and nonessential enzymes named Carol from Accounts Receivable. An office of one is more like a home office where the only interpersonal friction you can muster is between you and the Roomba (and Alexa, that know-it-all bitch). Learning to coexist in a mixed family of paid companions makes drama nearly unavoidable—especially when the team has to rely on one another to make money. Even the Bradys had drama, and I'm pretty sure no one in that family was being paid to be there—except Alice, who ironically got along with everyone.

In most cases, you will be the Alice: a position of servitude, a bad knee, and an obligation to mesh with a building full of people who seem deeply miscast. And truthfully, it's always going to be easier to know thine enemy and take your fifteen-minute break strategically to miss the regular meltdowns of personalities. Here's a field guide for how to handle the many coworkers you will encounter in your career.

TRIXIE: THE WORK HUSBAND / WORK WIFE

In real life, taking a husband or wife is a dated and emotionally lofty investment that rarely shows any return. At best, marriage is a transactional tax break. At worst? A way to control women and circumcise their freedom under God. However, in the workplace, a Work Husband / Work Wife is essential for survival. Loading fruit trucks at gunpoint in Kuwait can feel like a booze cruise in Branson when you have the right in-office support system. Any work environment is improved when there is someone you can corner in your cubicle to conduct a conversation of intense gravity about who ate the last muffin on Todd's desk or which intern left a hard, unflushable turd in the handicap stall. A strong work marriage is also a great way to dismiss your own poor conduct. With the Work Partner, it's important to become unyielding apologists for each other's worst behavior. Because let's be honest: *You* took the muffin, Denise. And what happened in the handicap stall was *not* the intern.

TRIXIE: THE BOOTLICKER / TRY-HARD / BOSS FAVE

Flattery will get you nowhere—*usually*. But that really depends on what kind of boss you have. If you have a normal human boss who is tethered to reality, use

flattery and try-hard behavior like a cowbell in rock music: cute for a taste, not for a swallow. However, we all know that the executive tiers of workplaces are full of individuals who have crossed over with John Edward. There are unique cases in which we are dealing with a Miranda Priestly who behaves more like a Madeline Ashton. *"Why, Miss Ashton! You look younger and younger every day!"* In those special cases, tragically, the Bootlicker will excel. The rest of us are stuck watching a live in-office rim job every morning. If you encounter a Bootlicker in the workplace, your scope of actionable recourse is rather limited. The boss will most likely begin to detect the sick syrup of flattery and peel away like lead paint in a nursery. Just wait it out under the table in the conference room . . . or embody the Aloof.

KATYA: **THE ALOOF**

This mysterious character is hard to pin down because of their near-total lack of presence in or around the workplace. The details of their personality are fuzzy, as are their name and title. Regardless, their stories all start the same: They graduated from their state school with a degree in communications, found an old lamp in the clearance section at a Bed Bath & Beyond, and took it home, rubbed it, and out of it floated a large flamboyant genie who, via a showstopping big-band musical number, granted their wish to have consistent, gainful employment without ever doing any work. They are averse to effort, allergic to responsibility, and impervious to cooperation. Their only consistent quality is their complete lack of interest in doing anything productive.

Since they clearly don't care about how they're perceived, they will only show any signs of life when their immediate livelihood is in question. Yes, much like trying to catch a family of raccoons living under your porch, you must bait your traps and prepare to strike. Depending on their interests, consider luring them with cash, food, or a hook. You must also, however, accept the reality that wild horses can't be tamed and lazy sloths won't be shamed. We live in a universe with infinite possibilities, but let's be honest: Chances are, in this reality you will never reach this person. And anyway, it seems like a lot of effort, doesn't it? Are you sure the destination will be worth the treacherous journey? Their avoidant nature makes it naturally difficult to approach or engage, so before you put any effort into this relationship, make sure that they are still alive, let alone still an employee of your workplace. It's not uncommon for your colleague to have died five years ago. Sometimes "out to lunch" means "dead."

KATYA: **THE NEPOTISM BENEFICIARY**

Before résumés, skills, habits, traits, or any of these pesky qualities that comprise an attractive applicant, we did things the old-fashioned way: by hoarding resources and distributing them only to our families. It's the same founding principle as the Italian Mafia's, and it's stuck around this long because we (falsely) assume that skills and talent are passed on through DNA. This is mostly due to a few standout examples where nepotism produced someone who was as good as, or even better than, their successful older relative. Despite her talents, if Sofia Coppola had been born into a family of nobodies in Iowa, she would probably be the assistant manager at a Victoria's Secret instead of a star filmmaker.

Nepotism gives every lucky kid a leg up, but it is especially a boon for the gravely stupid, the lazy, the incapable. Are you a dum-dum with no ambition who wants to do less than the bare minimum with results at breakneck speed? Consider being born into a family of successful individuals on the career path of your choice. If you are stuck working alongside someone whose interview took place at the family reunion instead of at the office, there are very few pieces of advice I can give you; nepotism kids are notoriously ballsy and do not fear authority. If you choose to attack, be careful. You might be met with an "Actually, Ellen, that's not true," and be stuck watching your whole world crumble beneath your feet. Life isn't fair.

TRIXIE: THE OFFICE SLUT

Now, some of you reading this are thinking, "This isn't me." But look at you: You're in a red patent leather pump and a sheer blouse with your nipples dimpling into the breezy fabric like Dixon Ticonderoga number two pencils. You're uncrossing your legs in back-seam sheer hosiery and you're about to sashay your two-hourglass figure down to the water cooler and inspire about twelve boners en route. You'll stop by the fresh-out-of-college Derek at reception and pretend you forgot how to use the fax again just so you can linger in an Academy Award–winning performance of a woman in distress. You'll slip in a puddle of precum on your way back to your chair, which is a birthday cake that you slowly lower your latex miniskirt onto. You just start moaning as soon as you sign into the Zoom meeting and you don't stop until you punch the clock at 5:00 p.m. If you don't think your workplace has an Office Slut, you *are* the Office Slut.

Speaking frankly, as long as sexual harassment is unchecked in the workplace, using your sexual allure to get what you want is fair game. Next time you want to Lean In® and ask for a raise, do it in some Agent Provocateur and turn the male gaze against the machine. You are the Office Slut, and you are the most powerful person on payroll. Do you need Friday off? Use the sexy-baby voice on Thursday. You want the company car? Xerox those titties and "accidentally" leave them on top of the recycling bin. Push for your own parking spot and then switch back to high turtlenecks and low ponytails until another issue arises. Rinse and repeat. If you'd like to hear a great story about using sexuality to disarm and parry, check out the anecdote about Tara from the salon in *Trixie and Katya's Guide to Modern Womanhood*.

TRIXIE: GRANDMOTHER WILLOW

There are some employees who truly find themselves unfireable. Nepotism or the elusive "being a good employee" might do the trick, but there is a longer game that is concrete and absolute: Be old. If you have worked at the business longer than the current higher-ups and their colleagues, you become a fixture as essential as central air and overhead fluorescents. I once worked with a server named Marlo who you would have believed laid the kitchen tile down herself in 1971. Marlo was a fabulous employee who was the fastest and most efficient server of any of us—*and* customers loved her. After clocking about twenty years at the restaurant, she was a great server as a matter of personal integrity. She wore a lemon-blond bubble ponytail down to her butt, which I believe is a food safety violation, but alas, the elderly are irreproachable. She could have mounted the hosting station, removed her uniform, and sprayed hot piss all over the menus while a family eating Cajun jambalaya watched and she probably wouldn't have even gotten a written warning. But she was great at her job, which is irregular for the Grandmother Willow.

There are more Grandmother Willow situations in the workplace where the elderly employee is far from exemplary. Crotchety, embittered, and typically a tattletale by nature, the Grandmother Willow can be your best friend or your worst enemy. All you can really hope for is that you remind her of her niece Jacqueline, or take a cue from the Bootlicker and feign genuine interest in her personal life. "Marlo, your husband has cancer? My sister *is a* Cancer! She was born on the Fourth of July!" Worst-case scenario, no one lives forever. However, they say retirement is the number one killer of the elderly, and as long as the Grandmother Willow is still picking up shifts on HotSchedules, you better get fountain bangs like Marlo's niece Jacqueline.

KATYA: THE OVERSHARER

She has no boundaries, she has no filter, she has no couth; the only things she seems to have are incredibly bad breath and very dry skin. There's no line she won't cross, and there's no hint she'll take. Since she clearly is not self-aware enough to pick up on your lack of interest or outright annoyance at her relentless gabbing, there is only so much I can advise you to do in terms of coping. I would encourage you to go through the stages of grief in response to the death of your inner peace. And once you get to that last step, acceptance, you must accept your circumstances and make the best of it by having fun! Lie! About everything! Tell her that your dad is a centaur and you are fluent in Gaelic. Tell her that you wrote the song "Bohemian Rhapsody" when you were a child and you sold it to Queen for ten bucks. There doesn't seem to be any reasonable, humane method of getting her to shut the fuck up, so use her presence to sharpen your craft of storytelling. If her chattiness is still unbearable, I have no choice but to encourage violence. This is not a job for HR, this is a job for MA, as in Sue Ann from the movie *Ma*. As a first line of defense, weaponize her chattiness against her by offering some extremely questionable details about your life, but desperate times call for desperate measures.

OFFICE LINGO

From Circling Back to Chiming In

BY TRIXIE

For some people, the shock of entering the working world is about more than just the harsh fluorescent overhead lighting. The office (the actual place, not the TV show, and, no, I don't care that you've seen the British version) is a social construct that relies on its inhabitants performing time-worn rituals and speaking in code, not unlike sorority initiation or *Rocky Horror*. Entering the office environment for the first time can feel like stumbling into a living art exhibition at MoMA that is supposed to be a "commentary" on "society" or a depressing, confusing, mistranslated foreign film. This is especially true for those of us whose education looked more like Torrance High School Cheerleading Team going to nationals than *Gossip Girl*. The upper class can't exist without its separation from the lower and middle classes; wealthy people are incentivized to make their world as insular and confusing as possible, so it can't be infiltrated. Don't let the diversity page on their website fool you. They will take ten idiot Kennedy offspring on name alone before they will read the second line of your résumé. If your parents don't have Wikipedia pages with sections like "Sailing Legacy" and "Insider Trading Controversy," you are automatically at a disadvantage.

If you're missing out on your leg up but still want to run with the big dogs, here is a crash course in translating the lingo of the office to help you on your journey.

Just circling back—This is, without exaggeration, the most malicious and ill-meaning attack one can sling at the office. It seems sweet and constructive, doesn't it? Almost disarming in its positive tone? Well, it really means, "Bitch, I shouldn't even have to be asking you twice, but if you don't do that shit I already asked you to do, I'm going to mount your desk and drop a deuce in your potted succulent while you watch."

Checking in on this!—I need that shit ASAP so I can move on with my sad life. And you dragging your feet on a basic task is making my life even sadder.

Hi, all—This isn't my job. So why am I the one organizing it? Only four of you are going to read this BS anyway.

I hope this email finds you well—I hope while you read this email your mother's body gets exhumed and kept on display at the Minnesota State Fair.

Best wishes—Eat shit and die, you pig fuck.

Nice to e-meet you!—You will never seem human to me until we meet in person and I am given reasons to like you.

Kindly—I've killed people before and eaten their skin.

Chiming in here—Sticking my nose in some shit that isn't my responsibility so I look busy but also petty.

No problem!—Yes, problem. Probably several, possibly across time zones and risking consequences in the tens or hundreds of thousands of dollars that will require me to not sleep tonight.

Colleague—Best judy, ride-or-die bitch.

Touching base—Being forced to interact with someone you are thankful is seated in a separate cubicle quad.

Put a pin in it—I cannot talk about this anymore but I'm afraid of quitting so I'll make it seem like this is a task I plan on returning to.

I don't have the bandwidth—I don't feel like doing this but I want you to think it's because I'm too busy when in fact I just can't do it without killing myself.

Noted—I hate you but I have to listen to you or at least make you feel like I listened to you.

Please advise—I'm fucking dumb.

Hope this helps!—Leave me alone.

Sorry for the double message—My Wi-Fi cut out because I am either broke or I have such a huge house that there are several competing routers.

Sent from my iPad—I'm extremely wealthy with my papyrus of the future. I'm also in bed watching porn.

I look forward to your reply—If you don't reply within twenty-four hours, I will infect your dog with rabies and wait for him to take your daughter.

ASKING FOR A RAISE

Bitch Better Have My Money

BY TRIXIE

Author Sheryl Sandberg famously inspired the masses with her book *Lean In*, where she encourages women to lead, inspire, and climb in the workplace. A major part of that lean is for more money, but leaning can be a tricky thing. A little leaning in a photograph, for example, can offset the obvious and unattractive length differential between your right and left legs. A little too much leaning can result in being hit in the face by a rogue pitching machine and having to get a bone graft on your face like my friend Tyler Fisher from middle school. The right amount of leaning in in the workplace, however, can help you skip rungs on the corporate ladder and come out rolling like Erika Jayne *before* the lawsuit.

But why are people so uncomfortable asking for a raise? We go back for a second or third plate at Old Country Buffet and never think twice about it, but when it comes to requantifying our elbow grease, we tend to recede faster than a gay man's hairline. When I worked hourly or salaried jobs, I never asked for a raise once or even pushed back on the first offer. Similarly, early in my entertainment career I never amended contracts or haggled over appearance fees. Why? Maybe a younger and more naive me was always thinking that I was being afforded the lion's share in the first offer. I also used to think that wrestling was real, so when it comes to my own brain's understanding of reality, I also never accept the first offer.

Looking back, I could not have been more misguided. Most employers aren't boundlessly generous. Best-case scenario, your employer isn't simply filling his or her day by willfully reexamining your salary, because other responsibilities are more pressing. Sadly, based on no data other than my disappointment in human compassion, that's probably not the case. Chances are your employer, like an extreme couponer with a basement full of laundry detergent and oatmeal, is looking to get the best deal for your labor. Ironically, you'll have to *become* an extreme couponer by necessity if you drift aimlessly into your salary figure. You stop short at second after putting a grounder into left field instead of trying to steal third base. (Sorry for the extended baseball reference, but I'm still thinking of Tyler Fisher's shattered cheekbone. He had to have a metal plate put in! We used to try to stick magnets to him at Boy Scouts until his mom found out.)

There are many reasons for raises, like a rising cost of living, promotions, relocation, and a good old-fashioned job well done. But even *no reason* is valid! There's never a danger in asking for more. My assistant, Brandon, goes to places that aren't even advertising any sort of sale or promotion and he will flatly ask for what he calls "the Hustler's Discount." It's a discount based on nothing for no reason and the gag is that he *regularly gets it*. Ten percent off here, cash back there, and all because he leaned in. Brandon is of course prepared to receive nothing extra, which is how you should feel asking for a pay adjustment. Become comfortable with the fact that your current salary's gestation period may not be complete yet in the eyes of your employer. You might feel uncomfortably pregnant with your new salary in the summer heat with swollen ankles, but your boss may insist that you are barely starting to show.

When it comes to asking for more money, I am always that bitch. And I am generous only in the interest of sharing information to help you also become that bitch. I have timelessly proclaimed that you should "know your worth and demand three times that." That's of course the bumper sticker version of a process that involves much more finesse. Here's a sort of pre–asking for a raise checklist to get you ready to pop the question.

HOW MUCH?

Before you enter your boss's office firing off compliments and smiling like a woman slipping into madness, we need to address how much you are going to ask for. First identify how much you currently make, and then decide how much higher makes sense. People traditionally ask for more than they believe they will actually get because that's how the process works. If you make ten dollars an hour and you're hoping for thirteen, ask for fifteen knowing that you will either work your way down to your goal or be pleasantly surprised by the boss's amenability. Going in with a number and being keenly aware of the multiple ways it could shake out is the best way to enter the renegotiation.

DO I DESERVE THIS?

Of course you "deserve" this, because the world is a magical place and good things happen to everyone, yada yada yada. But do you *really* deserve it? Have you completed every task with precision and efficiency? And most important, you should ask yourself this: "Am I making this company more money because of the way I do this job?" You're essentially asking your superior to allocate some of the company's profits to you. If you regularly find ways to save money, acquire and retain clients, and do the same job better than it was done before or could be done by other people, you stand on pretty firm ground for a raise, and chances are your superiors have noticed it. If this is you, slap on your tennis bracelet and get ready to secure the bag, sis.

Do you want a raise because you've been working there for a while now? Did you hear from Becky in HR that someone in your department makes more? Do you do your job? If these are your reasons for a raise, you're going to have to basically throw in a "World's Best Boss" mug and perform a triple axel on your employer's desk to get the conversation going because *you are currently doing the job you were paid to do in the way you were paid to do it.* You are the product, and your work has been sold by you for an agreed amount. Be careful reappraising yourself too fiercely or your boss might be reminded that there is a stack of résumés essentially comprising a phone book of equally satisfactory "products" who are only an interview away. Molly, you in danger, girl.

IS IT THE MONEY?

Listen, people like jobs for a lot of different reasons. For some, it's truly about the work. Maybe they like the mission statement or their colleagues. Liking the job for the money is also completely valid. However, if the job makes you want to retch and you fantasize about trapping the people you work with in a tanning bed with zip ties, the money may never be enough. Think critically about what your ideal workday is like and you will realize there are a lot of ways to get a "raise" without getting a dime. Perhaps part of asking for a raise should include asking for a more flexible schedule or a desk with a view. One day a week to work remotely, for example, might give you a day to decompress and keep everyone in the office safe from the impending tanning-bed scenario.

COLD HARD FACTS, DIANE

Nothing spells out "I'm worth more money than this" like a little bit of data. Have you become a more industrious employee? Prove it with Exhibit A. Your boss doesn't want interpreted tea leaves and gaseous theories; they want pie charts detailing the change in your worth and therefore your price. They want a spreadsheet that's been filled in using the lyrics to "Worth It" by Fifth Harmony. Show customer testimonials that you not only did your job, but you saved Baby Jessica from falling down the well and getting dismembered by gravity *while* saving the company a few hundred bucks on toner this quarter. "Because I did a good job" is a pretty subjective approach and can be argued. However, no one can argue with an Excel spreadsheet, bitch. Boot up that PowerPoint presentation and let those hos know.

There's of course definitely a reality where your renegotiation pays off and you walk away with a little more cheese than yesterday. Hooray! Congrats, my little baby girl. However, there is also a reality where your pitch falls flat, or the bag wasn't as secured as you thought it would be. Public crying, passive-aggressive Slack messages, and generalized spiraling are not the most poised recourse. Don't get bangs. Don't shirk responsibility in retaliation. Don't steal food from the fridge. In fact, recovering from a declined raise with grace is a fast way to impress your boss. Should you cry in the shower at home or get drunk at Applebee's after work? Definitely. Call up your girls and vent in a hefty "my boss is an idiot and my job sucks" monologue so that you can return to work on Monday with a vengeance.

The journey of a thousand calories starts with a single stolen yogurt from the work fridge.

GIRLBOSSES

BY TRIXIE & KATYA

What is a girlboss? Honey, if you have to ask, you aren't one. A true girlboss already knows and she is a princess of productivity, as well as a goddess of good ideas. She is opening her lotus flower and blooming across all social channels while guiding others to sign up for her women's wellness workshop. She's opening every interaction with "Why are you afraid of your own success?" and closing with "I don't have the bandwidth for that right now."

She is #UnapologeticAF while she's on her #WorkFlow. Humility is her hustle, gratitude is her grind, and her bread and butter consists of unchecked ruthlessness peppered with petty microaggressions, in spite of her lactose intolerance and aversion to carbohydrates. She works hard, she plays nasty, and it's always TGIF for this HBIC. How does she do it? Let's take a peek behind the gossamer curtain.

THE DAILY LIFE OF A GIRLBOSS

5:00 a.m.: Dawn simulator rouses me from my power sleep.

6:00: Scroll Goop, expel jade racquetball, repeat daily affirmations: *I am girl, I am boss.*

6:30: Peloton 2000s girl-power anthem ride with my favorite instructor, Cody Rigsby.

7:00: Breakfast: hard-boiled egg, half a grapefruit, warm bowl of stevia.

7:30: Insert tiger's-eye into bra.

8:56: Arrive on the roof of the nearby Nordstrom to hail my helicopter to Manhattan. It's four minutes flat. Change from my Vibram toe shoes into my studded Prada loafers.

9:00: Arrive at work; ask my receptionist what's holding her back today. Get everyone's name wrong on purpose.

9:30: Deny all of my employees' requests for time off while CoolSculpting.

10:00: Crisis management meeting where we create crises to manage.

10:30: Bagels in the conference room for the menstruating individuals of the office (we're all synced up!) for Freebleed Friday. Interpret the Rorschach patterns of our monthly gifts.

11:00: Trust falls off the second-floor balcony. Anyone afraid to jump is immediately fired.

12:00 p.m.: Write a beautiful calligraphy of the word "Girlboss."

12:30: Decide to change the spelling of my name from Annaleigh to Anna Lee; make my assistant order new stationery.

1:00: Working lunch at the Nordstrom Café with Suze Orman, Yoko Ono, Elizabeth Holmes, Christie Brinkley, and Taylor Swift's cats. Diet Cokes all around!

2:00: Solo tennis lesson in the lobby of the office to teach the team about spatial awareness. Scuff my Ked and then fire my receptionist for watching me do it.

3:00: Name-search myself in the company email server to find out if anyone has any opinions on my new bangs. Keywords: "boss," "bangs," "beautiful," "face-framing."

3:01: EMERGENCY meeting with my spiritual adviser in response to the lack of mention of my brave haircut.

4:00: Pull the office gay out of an important call to ask him what "stan" means, also if he has seen this week's *RHONY*. Tell him I think he's really brave, and to slay, queen.

4:30: FaceTime with my nanny and ask her to tell my newborn baby I love her in Spanish so she will grow up to be a bilingual badass girlboss.

5:00: Helicopter to Soho House for cocktails with the girls, Caitlyn Jenner and Meghan McCain.

6:00: TGIF! It's been a long week. Taking an Uber Black to JFK to fly home.

7:00: Seaweed wrap on my face, and my plate. Vegan vibes!

7:30: Zip up my Baby Phat tracksuit and head to our on-property sound-bath chamber for my nightly cathartic howl, followed by a light cry. It's so important to stay vulnerable as a woman in power.

7:45–8:00: DM Chrissy Teigen on my burner account.

8:00: Combine hot oat milk and six Ambien in my magic bullet for Mommy's Evening Elixir.

9:00: Arm my Ring, Nest, SimpliSafe, and bear traps to protect my home, before crawling into bed and watching the episode of *Glee* where Gwyneth Paltrow sings "Forget You" by CeeLo Green and fracking myself with my Hitachi until it blows out all the electricity on the property. Talk about lights-out!

Due to the egregious lack of female heads carved into large mountain ranges, we must create for ourselves the Mount Blushmore of our wildest motivational girlbossy dreams. Here is a selection of some notable entries in the *Girlbossipedia Britannica*.

Katya: Miranda Priestly

Let's kick it off strong and simple with a total fucking bitch. She's the unforgiving, uncompromising, unyielding, merciless, and unimpressible ultimate nightmare hag boss whose demands and expectations soar way beyond the capabilities of even the most skilled, attentive employee. She's the final boss at the end of the *Street Fighter Girlboss* video game. A giant, hideous wretch whose aversion to happiness is matched only by her lust for hate. She's the ultimate picture of frigid, shrewd, sexless female authority, complete with catchphrases and signature coif. She's the Third Reich in a silver swoopy hairdo, and her genocidal rage is directed toward incompetence and lack of taste. She's every gay masochist's *Mommie Dearest* fantasy. She doesn't waste her time with fleeting trivialities like happiness, joy, or laughter. If you asked her if it's lonely at the top, she'd look down on you and spit in your eye. Life is serious, work is tough, and if you ditch your loser sous chef boyfriend and fuck over your ingratiating coworker, you might get your hands on a pair of the Chanel boots.

Trixie: Jojo Siwa

Jojo Siwa is most definitely a girlboss. She was probably the first girlboss on record since she got famous on *Dance Moms* and then made enough money that she could buy and sell your whole family. Affluence isn't a measure of girlbossity, but extreme demonstrations of flagrant wealth are. Miss Siwa has a room in her home devoted to her own merchandise (Barbra Streisand's basement mall can pack it up, bitch), AND she has two (2) cars with her own face on them. Your face on your own car is a great way to advertise your small business, but it also makes it possible for first responders on the 110 to identify the body should you get decapitated. But a true girlboss like Jojo will never die. On top

of all this girlbossery, in 2021 she also let the world know that she was a member of the LGBTQIA+ community. For this reason, she could run over her own mother with her face-car and the community would have her back, spiritually and financially.

Trixie: RuPaul

The fabulous thing about girlbossing is that you don't even have to be a female—but it does help to dress like one on TV. RuPaul Charles has created a vibrant economy that ensures she is only ever viewed in her exact fantasy lighting. She has taken an art form that is based in physical beauty and materialism and commodified it as a gospel of self-love and acceptance. Brilliant! I have been to the RuPaul store in Hollywood and I drop dollars every single time. Why? Because the power of Miss RuPaul lets me know that I do in fact need a vinyl of a B-side track from 1996 and another dozen RuPaul candy bars. In all seriousness, the way Ru has married artistry and commerce is so inspiring to all queer people because you *can* be a creative and still get paid.

Trixie: Jill Barad

Ah yes, Jill Barad. Let me take you back: The year is 1997 and Mattel is the number one toy company in the world. Fourteen million girls in America own Barbie dolls—yet Mattel found through research that 80 percent of mothers believe that Barbie is a poor role model for girls. In the toy industry, you must of course entice the grubby, pudgy fists of children—that's a given. But more important, you must sell to the parents who ultimately have the almighty coin to spend. Take it from me: You're probably a youth reading this book right now who used Dad's credit card for this literary procurement. Thanks, Dad!

Enter Jill Barad, who was about to come through and change the world forever through a Barbie campaign slogan we still see used today: "We girls can do anything." These campaigns empowered young girls to imagine themselves on the moon, in the Olympics, and even in corporate America. For the first time, girls were invited to dream limitlessly. (I could be funny here, but when it comes to eleven-and-a-half-inch fashion dolls and the seismic impact they have on child development and therefore the world, I am more serious than a heart attack. I missed both my grandparents' funerals for doll conventions, and you know what? I never look back, honey.) Jill Barad was the CEO at Mattel from 1997 to 2000, at which point she was offered close to fifty million dollars in severance! Which means she was paid close to fifty million to never come back to work again. The gaggery and the true girlbosserina of this. I mean, her ultimate girl-who-is-a-boss move was to no longer be a female executive. LMAO. Gag.

Trixie: Randi Zuckerberg

Okay, this one is a little wild but please follow me here. I was once at an airport and I was feeling particularly overwhelmed. People often credit me as a woman who seems to be doing it all with a million babies in the bath at once, but I also live with the knowledge that at least one of those babies is drowning. I balance out this near-constant white noise of stress with frequent and public crying at the airport. One time I was choking on my own tears in the Delta Sky Lounge and a young girl came up to me and asked if I was okay. I wasn't. But on this exact layover where I was being slow-cooked by my own anxiety, I saw a book in a shop window called *Pick Three: You Can Have It All (Just Not Every Day)*. This self-help title penned by Mark Zuckerberg's sister called out to me like a meaty cross-dresser trying to hail a cab on a hot summer night.

Basically, Randi Zuckerberg says in the book that you have five general areas in life: family, work, sleep, fitness, and friends. Instead of choosing to focus on every area every day, you "pick three" to do well each day and live with the fact that being well-lopsided instead of well-balanced is the way to go. I'll admit that this could have stayed a concise tweet (I believe the impetus for this book was in fact a Randi tweet) or at most graduated to a "live laugh love"–style decal on the office wall of the regional manager of a Joann fabric store. I also love that a woman worth two hundred million dollars and whose brother owns Facebook believes she can relate to the average woman. A successful woman in the tech industry with a heavy dollop of delusion? *Big* girlboss energy over here, doll.

Katya: Carrie Bradshaw

Ambition is not the only driving force fueling the high-heeled strut of the contemporary girlboss, as week after hectic week of packed schedules can really throw a wrench into the modern woman's vibe. And thus, we turn to uptown girlboss role model Carrie Bradshaw, who enjoys all the luxuries of a high-powered Manhattan billionaire by only working about three hours a month. This sparse but lucrative time is spent perched at the open window of her brownstone, effortlessly tapping away on her laptop about various musings and pun-filled observations about her incredibly rich and multifaceted personal life, filled with brunch outings with the girls and daily thousand-dollar shoe purchases. Her allure is found not in the depth of her experience but in the completely outrageous science-fiction-level absurdity of a woman living in Manhattan and getting paid a hundred grand a month to write vaguely philosophical refrigerator magnet / fortune cookie / bumper sticker musings on the plight of being single. I can't help but wonder, is Carrie Bradshaw a girlboss or just a dumb bitch?

Katya: Sue Ellen Crandell

Crisis management is an essential feature in the job description and overall skill set of any girlboss. The ability to make the most out of a terrible plight is key, and this ability is on full glorious display throughout the critically undervalued, horrifically Oscar-snubbed, and incredibly compelling cinematic gem *Don't Tell Mom the Babysitter's Dead*. Right there in the title we find hiding in plain sight two key ingredients that help concoct the self-sufficient stew to nourish the burgeoning girlboss: lying and death. As Sue Ellen is faced with the harsh reality that her summer vacation will not be spent lounging at the beach with her friends but instead slaving away in a corporate hellscape to feed her helpless siblings when the babysitter dies, she does what any determined high school girlboss would do: fake a résumé, lie about her age, and assemble a meticulously power-clashing '90s wardrobe to land a gig at the executive level. She is the embodiment of the adage "Dress for the job you want." What does she want? She wants to be a Vassar girl who's right on top of that, Rose, delegating responsibility to others so she can finally get that forty-eight-hour orgasm.

Trixie: Elvira

Mama, we can't touch on the craft of girlbossing without visiting the Mistress of the Dark. Cassandra Peterson was basically the first mainstream drag queen and we love to see it. A young comedienne at the Groundlings, she auditioned for a shot-in-the-dark casting call as a new horror hostess on KHJ-TV. She combined the costume pitched by *Fright Night* and her Groundlings-developed Valley girl character and created a gold mine. Truly a sleeper agent of a businesswoman, she negotiated ownership of her own image and created dozens of licensed products: costumes, T-shirts, CDs, calendars, and even pinball machines. A woman in a wig with a knack for lucrative self-promotion? We have no choice but to stan this absolute Gurl Bausse.

Katya: Ma

Two letters, one syllable, and infinite possibilities: Ma. Dial *M* for murder and press *A* for Awesome. That's right, the scorned psychotic Sue Ann from the horror film *Ma* is a generous illustration of the darker shades and offbeat flavors of girlbossery. Ma is a woman with purpose, a lady with a plan, and a gal who just doesn't want to drink alone. She's just like us: All she wants at the end of the day is to be able to lay her head on the pillow next to the mutilated corpse of the man who wronged her in high school. Her hands-on, off-the-cuff, unconventional problem-solving skill set includes sewing up a mouthy bitch's lips, male strip shows at gunpoint, and canine-to-human blood transfusions. She faces her problems head-on and runs them over with a smile on her face. Her unassuming meekness conceals an unhinged volatility that has her buying you beer one minute and pumping your dad full of dog blood the next. She's a girl who has suffered but refuses to be bossed around by her trauma. And if the whole town has to go up in flames for her to get what she wants, then we'll all be laughing in Hell together.

Katya: Tess McGill

With "a head for business and a bod for sin," Melanie Griffith's iconic Tess McGill is the ultimate Cinderella story for late '80s capitalism, and of course her story inspired the title of this very helpful and informative book. She dresses for the job that she wants by stealing the dress that she needs. She'll stop at nothing in order to get what and who she wants, namely, a corner office and Harrison Ford's giant dong.

Tess is a lone she-wolf who uses her giant wings to soar above her competition by flying under the radar. She perseveres in spite of the complete and total lack of support from any woman in her life—even her best friend pleads with her to wise up, get real, and face the facts: that she's just another dumb bitch from Staten Island who should just marry the guy who cheated on her three days ago. The tension between Tess and her boss, Katharine, is a sad but realistic illustration of what economists refer to as the McGill-Parker effect: If two intelligent, beautiful women are up for the same position in a company, one of them will get promoted while the other will get their legs broken in a skiing accident. Critics might call Tess insane, but she's really just a maverick, a daredevil, a humdinger. She's not afraid to crash a socialite's wedding, or to juggle more than three aliases, all in service of making it big in the corporate world. She doesn't play by the rules, mostly because she doesn't know what the rules are, but who cares—it was surely some dipshit man who made them up anyway.

Katya: Add Your Own!

The possibilities are nearly infinite. I suggest beginning with people whose names start with G or B. Like Gina or Beth.

While this list is impressive, it is far from comprehensive. New girlbosses are being indoctrinated every few minutes, while former girlbosses are being ushered into cushy retirement at SoulCycle and Charming Charlie. At the closing of this chapter, it's important to reinforce that being a girlboss has nothing to do with being female or being in a position of power. It's about state of mind, self-image, and knowing that when you get out of bed in the morning, you possess a gorgeous set of breasts. See you on Slack!

MANAGEMENT STYLES

Manage-à-trois

BY KATYA

The word "manage" brings up a variety of associations. Time management, crisis manager, managing to shoplift three iPads by shoving them in your sweatpants; these all come to mind immediately. In the workplace, "management" is an umbrella term encompassing the hierarchy of people who make the official decisions regarding money, rules, hiring, and firing. Management has final say on all developments within the company. While the president of the United States has checks and balances from the other branches of the federal government to curb their power, the general manager of a franchised Taco Bell is bound by no such restrictions.

As a manager, you must consider your strategy for making the high-pressure, impactful game-time decisions that your company has entrusted you to make. I am so pleased to have been given the unique responsibility of guiding you on this journey.

Just like a cult, an office is nothing without a strong leader. A good boss can nurture their subordinates and lead the team to boundless success. A bad boss can slowly bleed the life-force from the office environment like a gangrenous limb. The fitness of a leader is often measured by ridiculously arbitrary distinctions like accolades, IQ, alma mater, and Myers-Briggs type. These are all meaningless. Nobody has ever gotten anywhere by being balanced and rational. The best leaders, the ones who have been immortalized by history, led with style.

If you find yourself in a position of leadership, your first order of business should be to figure out your leadership style. Who will you embody? What will your story be? You might want to compile anywhere from one to five vision boards. Inspiration can strike from anywhere! Ask the most trusted members of your inner circle who you remind them of. Ask your lover(s) what energy you emit sexually. Find out which celebrities and entrepreneurs have the same zodiac sign as you. Also, while you're asking around, find out what the soup of the day is at Olive Garden today.

You also should figure out the aesthetic of your regime. Which colors, textures, or motifs best represent you? Red is a classic color that communicates power and passion and a little bit of fear, which is great for a leader. But don't lose touch with your own identity and personal style. Many empires also have an object or animal that signifies their message—donkeys for the Democratic Party, tigers for the Black Panthers, etc. What comes to mind for you? The possibilities are endless. These factors will all help you refine your managerial style and create your compass for corporate decision-making.

If you're looking for a jumping-off point for your tenure as a leader, I have compiled some of the best time-tested leadership styles that will lead any office to success.

THE 5 ZAMOLODCHIKOVA-APPROVED LEADERSHIP STYLES

The *Basic Instinct* Management Style

All thrills, no frills, no bra, and no panties. Psychosexual mind games, uninhibited bisexuality, silk scarves, and serial murder all come together, pun intended, to make this management style perfect for keeping your subordinates on their

toes. You should be maniacally obsessed with your employees and they should be seduced by you as a leader. This cat-and-mouse leadership style demands their focus at the office, which doubles as a bedroom. This managerial mode is often confused with its sister style, "The *Illicit Confessions* Management Method," which is literally just having lots of sex at work.

The Italian Mafia Management Style

Blood may be thicker than water, but pasta is chunkier than money. In this old-world management style, family rules everything. Contracts are uttered in darkened backroom offices, and deals are sealed with a wet signature in Ma's gravy. Your employees must defer to you with the utmost allegiance and loyalty, so much so that anyone who dares

to fuck with you should say good-bye to their fingers. This management style encourages creativity and utilitarianism in the team: They will learn creative ways to dispose of bodies, and also how to turn a broom closet into an interrogation room. This management style encourages the team to compartmentalize their emotions, which is excellent for productivity. Gabagool and pasta fagioli served in the cafeteria every day!

The Russian Mafia Management Style

See above, but swap Ma's gravy for sour cream and lower the temperature thirty degrees.

The *Purge* Management Style

This management style was designed to combat the troubling power structures that often plague traditional workplaces. Every third Thursday, the positions completely shake up and the employee handbook is tossed out the window. Janice from the mailroom becomes the CEO today, and Olga from the lunchroom is suddenly VP of finance. Ted from HR is cleaning the toilets. Traditionally, the executive

board also leaves their houses unlocked and their car keys in the garage. This encourages equity and open communication between the bosses and employees.

The *Eyes Wide Shut* Management Style

Work should be seductive, like sex, but also mysterious, like life. This management style turns the humdrum boring office landscape into a masqueraded orgy full of password-protected sex rituals accessible only by limousine. The team is bound by secrecy and shared knowledge of the filthy acts they have committed together, and post-work conviviality is enhanced by everyone having been married to Nicole Kidman. When the workplace is a menacing Kubrickian environment that demands perfection and innovation, the output will be a modern masterpiece, give or take a few dead hookers.

If you follow these methods, you should expect nothing less than extreme success and unflappable synergy. Profits will likely quadruple if not quintuple, and you will have an office of employees who experience the highest levels of satisfaction and euphoria at work. The most qualified individuals in your industry will be lining up in droves to interview for your company, and you will probably become very rich and handsome, too. You are not a flop.

I also feel compelled to remind you of the famous saying "There is such a thing as too much of a good thing." Have you heard that one? Well, whoever said that is an idiot and wrong. Go get drunk with power, and make sure you drink some water before your head hits the pillow so you don't wake up with a hangover.

WORKING REMOTELY

When The Boardroom Is Your Bedroom

BY TRIXIE

We are very fortunate to be a part of the rat race at a time when much of the cheese chasing can happen in a virtual office. Gone are the days of shuffling into the office at 9:00 a.m. on a Monday only to pretend to work for the first several hours. Now you can pretend to work from home! Many studies have shown that the COVID-19 pandemic changed the office as we know it forever and that if Michael Scott were a character created today, most of his "that's what she said" quips would have been communicated via Zoom.

When working remotely, it's up to you to decide whether you're going to be a pig of productivity or a sloth of sloven. You could get up early, exfoliate, and

put on some olive chinos. You could do three hundred crunches while navigating your emails and forwarding office jokes to your coworkers. You could run laps around your colleagues on Slack and end the day promptly at 5:00 p.m. by closing your laptop with satisfied decorum. Or (and more likely) you can slip into a stream-of-consciousness improv exercise of pretending to work. You can log on to the company server and move the mouse just often enough to appear "online." You can chime in on email chains with simple TGIF-style one-liners. Or, my favorite: You can even make up questions about the project you are working on as a subtle way to assure the virtual office that you are knee-deep in hog-shit paperwork and struggling only to meter your own ambition.

The only challenge here is that keeping up a convincing charade of pretend work can be just as taxing as actual work, at which point, if you work for me, I hope you quit. I'm all for time theft until it's my company. When it's my corporate dollar, I only expect you to step off the hamster wheel to get my coffee. And I don't even drink coffee.

Men's Health magazine told me that virtual offices are the future. This claim was supported by COVID restrictions lifting in 2021 and businesses deciding not to rent empty rooms for no reason. In the likely event that you find yourself shouting, "I'm right on top of that, Rose," to no one other than your succulents, here's some guidance on how to be the employee of the month without ever setting foot in the office.

CREATE A HOME OFFICE ENVIRONMENT THAT PROMOTES PRODUCTIVITY

A. *A Room of One's Own* **vibes.** The value of having your own space to be productive in cannot be overstated. Maintaining a space that inspires you and keeps you focused is essential to yada yada yada . . . Let's be honest here, Deborah. We all work better in a space we like, which makes one wonder how cubicles ever helped anyone. I had a cubicle only once. It was gray, plain, and claustrophobic. I was elated to be fired for doing puff-paint artwork on the clock (see the chapter

"Getting Fired"). I recommend natural light, a brisk temperature, and some ambient yet not distracting music. Even now as I write this chapter, I am listening to the *Valley of the Dolls* music from the motion picture LP. Its hypnotic tracks are fast-acting, like a work-appropriate quaalude. I'm here working, yet I feel transported and safe.

B. Minimize distractions. This is where not having children, pets, or roommates is key. Unwanted distractions cannot be a part of your work terrarium. Distractions are dripping boners from the devil full of lust and expended seed. Don't get seduced by the desire to do things that aren't what you are supposed to be doing. I am currently typing at a computer in my office that has the Wi-Fi disabled because I can't be trusted to not open a new tab and shop Gucci or peruse some FTM porn. My desire to buy a tracksuit and financially support the trans OnlyFans community is strong, but my drive to finish this clunker of a book must remain stronger.

ZOOMS—SEEM THE MOST PREPARED BUT DO THE LEAST

A. Pants? For who, society? One of the big bonuses of working remotely away from the office is also working remotely away from your pantaloons. Imagine engaging in the sizzle of word processing and "just circling back" emails with bare bottoms. The truest thrill is being on a Zoom half-naked. The Pacific breeze dancing across your ample bush as you say, "Just to echo what was said earlier," and stare at your own camera the whole meeting. There's something exciting and forbidden about being half-naked on the clock, but the rush doesn't come without caution. There's always the looming threat of slipping a nut on Zoom.

B. Pretend paying attention. "What's that? Oh, sorry, you cut out." That's what I've said every time I've ever snapped back into reality after spacing out on a Zoom. The Wi-Fi connection was fine; I was simply not tethered by the conversation being engaged in by the group. Gooning into the airspace and letting your mind wander is a natural part of workflow. Embrace it! Just have some finesse when you inevitably have to pretend you were listening the whole time.

C. Cope with technical difficulties. (Listen, no one expects you to be a member of the Geek Squad. Unless of course you work at Best Buy at the Geek Squad counter, in which case skip this section.) Loss of sound, dropped camera feeds, and assorted tech flops are part of the home office experience. Look on the bright side: When you work from home already instead of going into the office, tech hiccups can be your new fake sick day. "Sorry I couldn't be on the call earlier. My iPhone, iPad, and MacBook all exploded right when I sat down to join the conference. I'm currently picking broken glass out of my hair and trying to stop the bleeding. When I put out the fires, I'll follow up. TGIF!"

D. Microsoft Teams? Electric chair. Point-blank period. I hate this app so much. I had it installed for a corporate gig and it automatically pops up every time I boot up the computer. With no information on how to remove it, I'm considering identity theft or faking my own death. Ironically, an app called "Teams" is a great way to dismantle a functioning network of colleagues.

MANAGE TIME EFFECTIVELY

A. Without Deb from Accounting cracking her knuckles every twenty minutes on the dot, how can you keep track of time? Without proper time management, the day can slip away from you and you can find yourself several ten-milligram-edibles-deep trying to meet deadlines you should have squared away by noon. Time is money, and poorly managing your time is poorly managing your money. You owe it to yourself to complete tasks efficiently at the beginning of the morning so you can spend the majority of the day focusing on pretend work: paperclip necklaces, office pranks, and gossiping by the water cooler. Unfortunately for you, the employee working from home, gossiping by the water cooler is standing with the fridge door open talking to yourself.

WORKPLACE WELLNESS

It's a Jungle in There

BY KATYA

I hope this email finds you well." As Trixie mentioned, many members of the contemporary workforce are no doubt familiar with this greeting, which is not so much a greeting but rather an ominous portent of a hideously burdensome task that is all but guaranteed to extract any remnants of a soul left in your body as quickly as Uma Thurman snatched out Daryl Hannah's last good eye in *Kill Bill*. I have such a distaste for email, even though I fully acknowledge its utility and the necessity of instant, paperless long-form communication. Call me old-fashioned, but I actually yearn for what is now referred to as "snail mail," which I find to be a slanderous indictment of the postal service, one of the few modern institutions that I not only revere but absolutely adore (the others are telephone booths and public libraries).

Consider for a moment that your loving husband has died. Which of the following scenarios would you prefer? Option 1: You open your laptop, and in the blinding bluish-white screen of your inbox you see, sandwiched between an ad for Bed Bath & Beyond and a coupon for the Container Store, an email from "sender unknown" with the subject line "PLS READ: re: husband DEAD"; or Option 2: You are lounging on the porch in your red gingham nightgown, puffin' on a Lucky Strike as a military truck pulls up to your farmhouse. An officer exits the vehicle with a letter, the contents of which you already know, as the horrible news is apparent in the solemn gait of the officer, into whose arms you collapse, and as his broad musculature provides the virile scaffolding for your grief-stricken, nubile body, you are unable to resist the undeniable attraction that takes you both by surprise; one thing leads to another, and the memory of your dearly departed husband and his untimely death fades in the scorching embrace of a new and wild and utterly forbidden love. In short, email sucks.

In this day and age, the chances of an email finding you well are, well, not that likely. Considering the myriad ways the contemporary work environment is designed to inhibit health, it's just as likely that that email will find you at the bottom of a well, or simply not at all, because you are dead, on account of having thrown yourself into a well. Well, there's good news and bad news. Let's start with the bad, as that seems to be in line with the tone thus far.

Working forty hours or more a week in an office can kill you. I'm not being dramatic or hysterical, and I'm not necessarily trying to scare you into quitting your job (I'll try that in the "Quitting" chapter). I'm merely reporting to you what many scientists, most clergymen, and a handful of elite athletes have known for centuries: that the human body was not meant to sit still and do nothing. *Tell that to my deadbeat husband,* I can hear you screaming. Don't worry, I will, but in the meantime, please, listen.

From an evolutionary-biological standpoint, our species evolved slowly over many decades from less intelligent and much hairier primate ancestors. It took forever before the first primate species came down from the trees, stood upright, and began walking with just the back pair of hands, which would eventually be known as feet. So how did those feet end up squished into a pair of Nine West clompers concealed by a standard-issue office desk, inhabited by the pallid creature known as the modern office worker? How did we, as a species, go from "ooga booga" to "chiming in"? The modern business model is a satanic ritual, and your body is the sacrifice.

The decline of worker well-being can be traced back to a moment in history I'm sure you all remember from school. It was back in 1804, when Marie Curie and Sally Field were enjoying mimosas in a pied-à-terre in Paris and two apples fell down on their heads, kicking off what is now called the Industrial Revolution. It wasn't long until factories began employing children, and later adults because the kids needed someone who could buy them alcohol.

Now, here we are. The reality of worker wellness is bleak, and if my prose isn't enough to convince you of this, just look at the statistics.

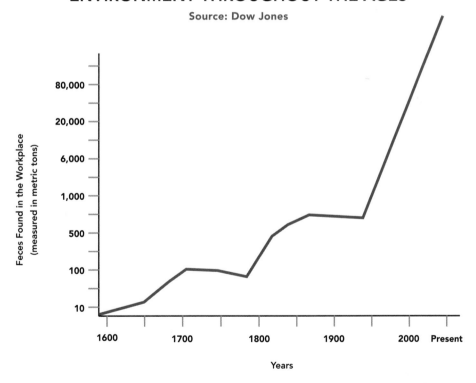

Fig. 1: Just look at this line graph showing the staggering growth in the amount of human feces found in and around offices from the year 1600 to now.

DEATH IN THE OFFICE

Source: Marcia Gay Harden

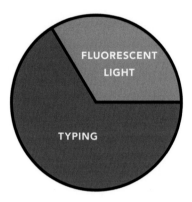

Fig. 2: This pie chart shows the causes of death for humans of all ages. Far and away, the lion's share of deaths are caused by typing-related injuries, and the second-largest contributor to death is fluorescent overhead lighting.

CORRELATION BETWEEN USE OF GMAIL AND CERTAIN DEATH

Control group also given heroin and crack and guns

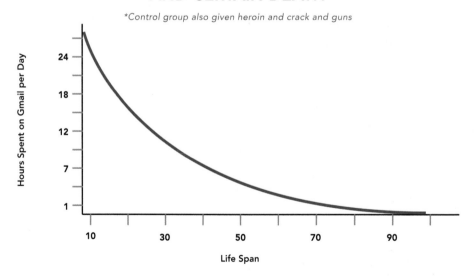

Fig. 3: The positive correlation between early death and time spent on Gmail is no joke and should be taken just as seriously as heart failure, AIDS, and feline diabetes.

There's no way around it: We are in a crisis. Birth rates in offices are at an all-time low. And studies are showing that people who work in offices and drink windshield wiper fluid die on average thirty-five years earlier than people who don't drink windshield wiper fluid. Beyond these crucial somatic health markers, the psychological wellness of the office worker is not at all where it should be. And the proof is in the pudding. Just look at the greatest minds of history—did Socrates sleep with his phone next to him in bed, with the ringer turned on? Did Nietzsche get wrist cramps from typing on his MacBook Pro? Of course not.

I'm not the first person to notice this phenomenon. Silicon Valley has tried to combat workplace ailments with futuristic devices like cryogenic reverse-gravity bathrooms and mandatory hourly biodynamic Kegels. But these interventions have only worsened our problems. The truth is, we do not need to make more "things" to solve our problems. In fact, we need fewer. If we want to reclaim the vitality and strength of our Paleolithic predecessors, we need to live like them. It's time to turn the office into the jungle.

The look and feel of the office is a far cry from the expansive terrain inhabited by cave people. We need to take drastic measures.

Private bathroom stalls must be converted into communal open-concept excretion zones. Don't you hate your office's single-ply toilet paper? Me too. That's why we're switching them out with banana leaves, or, to cut costs, the most accessible tools in the world: leftie and rightie.

Fluorescent lighting is basically 9/11 for the eyes, Hiroshima for the skin, and the *Hindenburg* for the nervous system. Florence Nightingale, who invented fluorescent lighting, was an avid hater of daylight and swore vengeance on the sun after she caught her husband, Terrence Nightingale, in broad daylight stark naked in a phone booth trying to call collect to vote on *American Idol*. It was later determined that Terrence's vote sealed the fate of beloved American sweetie David Archuleta, who would then go on to make an ill-fated turn as Sarah Jessica Parkour in the short-lived and much-maligned Broadway flop *SeX-Games and the City*.

It's no wonder such a vile invention born of spite and hatred would serve as the guiding light for American capitalism. But anyone with half a brain knows

120

that it's time for a big girl to win, that big girl being the sun, of course. Offices, schools, and hospitals around the country would do well to widen their doorways and reinforce their runways, because this plus-size diva is coming not just for the lights, but for the clocks, 'cause she runs on her own time and it's high time we all follow her lead. That's right, we're taking out all artificial lighting and subscribing to the werk schedule of the sun. If she's not out, neither are we. When the sun sets, it's scalpels down and tiddies out. No exceptions. Much to the chagrin of those at the North and South Poles. Y'all are on your own.

Abolition of the uniform and the dress code—this has produced mixed results, and it's easy to see why. In a longitudinal study, results showed that offices without dress codes experienced a degree of chaos that led directly to a staggering increase in feces, both in and around the designated excretion zones. By contrast, however, a latitudinal study showed that offices with stricter dress codes saw the same increase, but in animal feces only. Either way, it appears, dressing for the job that you want or have is just bullshit.

The exchange of money for goods and services is the clearest and most vibrant indicator of moral and social decline. Consider the country of Japan. They stopped using money in the late '80s, and by 1992 it was estimated that more than 70 percent of the population had become furiously bisexual. Such a radical overhaul of the financial sector is highly unlikely in the United States, but there is still some hope. According to *New York Times* bestselling economist Ann Dow Jones, replacing stocks with stockings, and swapping NFT with HRT (that's hormone replacement therapy, hunty) not only would cause a dramatic shift toward economic equality but would also bolster the struggling market for lacy unmentionables.

While this chapter may not have found you well, I hope you can at least feel a little good knowing that it's virtually impossible to be healthy in the modern workplace. But there is yet a shard of light in the bottom of the well—and speaking of which, to quote the great American hero Baby Jessica, "Modern life is often a mechanical oppression, and liquor is the only mechanical relief."

ANGELS AND DEVILS IN THE WORKPLACE

BY TRIXIE & KATYA

TRIXIE: ANGEL IN THE WORKPLACE— HOW TO BE GOOD AT WORK

- Always come in on time and offer to stay late. Being on time is the easiest way to make a huge impact in the workplace. Stuck in traffic? Nothing says, "I'm right on top of that, Rose," like veering onto the shoulder and jumping the median to make it to work on time. Pro tip: Allow time to clean the human teeth and hair out of your grille before screeching into the "Employee of the Month" spot.

- Be one step ahead, always on the lookout for potential complications in the future. Bosses don't like it when challenges are presented as dead ends. They like to hear about a succinct impediment that's in the rearview and the effective fixes that were already implemented before lunch break. It sounds corny as hell, but every snag at work is an opportunity to show your superiors how their employee can Frogger across the highway of administrative adversity and come out the other side unsquashed.

- Try to establish friendly rapport with your coworkers. "Hey, Beverly, can you believe it's Monday already? Where did the weekend go!" You don't even like Beverly. You think she smells like

noodles and wears ugly scarves that completely castrate her neckline from the side profile. But it's easier to establish some sort of rapport so that when the rapture (downsizing) comes, you have someone to voice your concerns to via text. It might even be worth laying on some flattery: "Your scarf is fake Gucci? Why, Beverly, I would have never known! You're so chic and clever and you don't smell like noodles!"

- Take organized, succinct notes at every meeting using your best pen. Pen choice tells you everything about someone. Ballpoint Bic? Played out. Quill? Try-hard. Gel pen? A hot slut who doesn't have the extra calories to expend to drag a metal tip across paper. She needs to glide and slide her way up the corporate ladder in a rainbow of metallic finishes. (See "The Office Slut" in the "Types of Coworkers" chapter.)

- If your workplace has a kitchen / snack table, make it a special treat for when you really need it. Also, always restock what you take and be courteous with trash. Mary, no one wants to step into the communal kitchen and for a moment believe they stumbled into Osama bin Laden's spider hole. Stealing food is a sign of weakness, like vaping or smiling. And don't treat your workplace snack bowl like an Old Country Buffet. Being caught on security footage smuggling fifteen Diet Cokes into your Mazda isn't going to bode well at your quarterly review.

KATYA: DEVIL IN THE WORKPLACE— HOW TO BE BAD AT WORK AND NOT GET FIRED

- Time is a flat circle. Time is a construct. Time is an illusion. Time is open to interpretation. That's why I suggest you show up an hour late every day and blame traffic even though you don't have a car. Always take a two-hour business lunch. And leave an hour and a half early—to beat traffic, obviously. Brilliance doesn't adhere to the standard workweek. Genius is strangled by rigid time constraints. Do you think Sir Isaac Newton discovered gravity by promptly punching his time card at the physics factory? No, he realized that gravity, just like time, is governed by forces beyond our control that we can attempt (in vain) to understand. Imagine: If he had been so diligent and punctual, he probably wouldn't have had that relaxing moment when the apple fell on his head, providing a lightning-flash insight that made him realize the truth about how apples and other objects languishing above the ground tend to fall under the pressure of some undiscovered force. The ancient Greeks might have attributed the sudden and curious dropping of fruit and other substantial objects toward the ground as some mysterious plot or calculated long-form trolling, but the Roman Empire got involved and eventually determined that the falling apple motion mystery was likely due to religious dogma.

- Avoid all responsibilities by presenting yourself with childlike innocence. And I suggest you take this to the extreme. I'm talking nonverbal baby noises. Youth is overvalued in the industry, after all. Betty Boop should be your role model here. When confronted by your boss, consider trading your expansive professional vocabulary for some simple vowel sounds. Instead of rattling off excuses, try this simple motto: "Boop boop be doop." Widen your eyes, shrivel up your mouth to an opening incapable of more than two syllables, and coo like a baby who is watching a spoon of applesauce. You can even dress like a baby if you need to. Nobody can fire a baby. They're probably scared of violating labor laws. Plus, family first.

- Never let your coworkers know anything about you. When they ask you questions about your life, change up your story every time to perpetuate an air of mystery. Having a job is like being arrested:

Anything you say can and will be used against you. Go light with the details, be vague in your descriptions, and don't be afraid to cry. If you feel like things are too personal, just start crying, and then immediately laugh. And then yawn. Like a baby (see above).

- Practice Duolingo on your phone during every meeting. It's very fun. This isn't sponsored. Fifteen minutes of language learning a day can change your life. Imagine what forty-five minutes during a boring quarterly one-on-one meeting could do.

- Work kitchen? Did you say an endless all-you-can-eat buffet? Food is meant to be eaten, and drinks are meant to be drunk. These are the laws of the kitchen. Different cultures approach food differently. There's no reasonable expectation for you to abide by the rules of the workplace kitchen or common space. First come, first served. We were all hunters and gatherers once, so it's your evolutionary duty to forage pretzels from the snack room. And if a person goes out of their way to label and protect their food, that just means they have boundaries they need to break down. What better way to teach them a lesson about the futility of preserving half an egg salad sandwich? Calories cannot be controlled, only consumed. Don't be afraid to put your straw in their drink too. Sharing is caring.

PART THREE

LEAVING YOUR JOB

/CAREER
SITIONS

FIRING SOMEONE

It's Not Me, It's You

BY TRIXIE

With great power comes great responsibility—and that "responsibility" is crushing souls. I learned this lesson firsthand when I had to let go of the first employee of my makeup company over the phone. I tried to defuse the situation by doing a funny voice, but I got hung up on.

Unless you are a sick freak who takes pleasure in stripping someone of their employment, you probably dread the idea of firing someone. But the truth is that firing someone is often in the best interest of the company and, more important, the people who work for it. Remember when Roseanne was fired from *Roseanne*? I, the enthusiastic viewer, couldn't have imagined the show without our fearless yet Twitter-illiterate Roseanne. Lo and behold, three seasons into *The Connors* I have come to forget that this family once orbited around a problematic nut farmer.

Before we start, let's get some terminology set. I don't know how everyone feels about the term "let go," but I am not living for it. This term is typically meant to soften the blow and avoid the big f-word (not "fag," but "fired"). But let's not oversoften; this is someone's job, Mary. Not Adele Dazeem belting out her song from *Frozen* at the Oscars.

I understand as a CEO that there's a difference between getting "fired" and being "let go," but I feel like there should be a better word for when you don't work somewhere anymore because they couldn't pay you anymore. Being "Old Yeller'd" can be for when you're being murdered as you leave the office. Being "Becky Connor'd" can be for when you are being replaced by someone because you are going to college. "We are letting you go" radiates an impersonal chill and is a term that really means nothing and anything. Whose job was it to come up with that term? I picture a weathered gay intern at a WeWork sweating over a MacBook before finally lofting out "let go." Maybe he should be "let go."

Is it your first time in this situation? Maybe you're a cutthroat girlboss (see the "Girlbosses" chapter) business bitch who's finally shattered the glass ceiling and made it to the top after years of hustling. You're strutting into the office with a match, some gasoline, and a list of men's names. Or maybe you're a twenty-five-year-old white guy who walked through the door of a tech startup literally yesterday and instantly got paid five hundred thousand a year and you're ready to see some heads roll. But no matter who you are, if you're on the fence about giving someone the chop, fear not! I have created a helpful guide to walk you through this challenging process. We're gonna figure this out together!

SIGNS IT'S TIME TO FIRE SOMEONE

Consistent Poor Performance

I know this is a joke book, but the first thing you should really do if your employee's performance slips is make sure that everything is okay, because it could be a sign that something in their life is affecting their job performance. Maybe their dog forgot their birthday. Maybe their favorite person went home on *The Voice.* Maybe the specter from the attic has become more daring and started wearing her Manolos without asking. That being said, if they just fumbled through the door on day one and have sucked since, maybe that's a sign that this job isn't the best fit for them. (It's also a sign that you need to sharpen your hiring process.)

Frequent Rule Breaking

Breaking the rules is very common in this day and age. Just the other day I ran a red light and hit a woman wearing white shoes after Labor Day. As her cream loafers bounced off the hood of my Chrysler, I offered a simple "You know what you did!"

If everyone paid their taxes the way they're supposed to, the United States would look like Santa's workshop on December 26. Cool, collected, and little people having sex on Xerox machines. Lots of rule breaking is commonsense and easily dismissible, which is fine because a *Handmaid's Tale* society isn't ideal either. A rolling stop is only a problem on the day of your driving test and when you've pulled out of Starbucks recklessly and squashed a French bulldog. But there is definitely a difference between going twenty-seven in a twenty-five and showing up forty-five minutes late every day, stealing from the cash drawer, and telling people to go fuck themselves on your work email.

They Won't Stop Showing You Pictures of Their Kids

Inexcusable. Parents, I'm talking to you. If we work together, I don't ever want to be made aware of your children. No one is impressed, and no one cares. No one has ever cared. Every moment you spend detailing the pitfalls of parenthood is tiny shallow cuts all over my body. Especially if you have LGBTQIA+ coworkers, please leave us out of your sad life of Pampers and Goldfish crackers.

So, you've decided that it is indeed time to hand them their pink slip. Congrats! Or should I say I'm sorry? If you're a true sadist, I guess "Have fun!" I never get these things right. Regardless, you should beware of these common mistakes that are often made during The Conversation.™

WHAT *NOT* TO DO WHEN FIRING SOMEONE

Leave the Reason for the Meeting So Ambiguous They Don't See It Coming

So simple, yet so frequently mishandled. Don't make them think that this meeting is for something, literally anything, else. As far as you know, the employee knows nothing of the twisted fate that has been set upon them. Whether it's over email or in person, add a sprinkle of urgency and seriousness to the tone of your invite. "Hi, Beverly! Stop by my office for a girls' happy hour! P.S. Wear waterproof mascara." If it's IRL, rehearse in the mirror. Do a couple sense-memory acting exercises and really drop into the scene. If they come into your office and think the meeting is about what to get Jennifer from HR for her birthday lunch, you're fucked. You're asking for an after-lunch scream match with Renee from Sales. As the potted succulent flies across your desk and smashes on your framed college degree behind you, you'll wish you had added a "P.S. This is about your future with the company" to the email.

Beat around the Bush

Just rip off the Band-Aid. Nothing good comes from avoiding the subject. Look the temp straight in the eyes and say, "Listen, Daryl or Deidre or whoever you are, it's not working. And now you're not working. The Coffee Bean by my house is hiring but beware: I go there every morning and if you thought I was a difficult boss, wait until you see what kind of customer I am."

Make Someone Else Be the Messenger

This one's a toughie. Being as direct as possible when breaking the news is, in general, the best move. Remember when Joe Jonas dumped Taylor Swift over a twenty-seven-second phone call and everyone hated him for it? I don't remember that, but a girl who works for me loves Taylor and told me about it. Putting barriers between you, the firer, and them, the firee, is only going to make you look bad (as it SHOULD, tbh). However, if you don't care about dignity or respect, it's acceptable to take a half day and make Shanice from HR commence the bloodletting.

Accidentally Call Them "Mom" at the Beginning of the Meeting

There's no going back from that. I guess that person has to work for you forever now, sorry! You two will probably grow old together and have a joint retirement party with a picture of both of you on the cake. You have now created a Grandmother Willow as addressed in our field guide to coworkers.

Here's a quick pop quiz for comprehension:

WHAT IS THE BEST WAY TO FIRE SOMEONE?

a. Schedule a meeting on their birthday; serve cake.

b. Spend the first forty-five minutes telling them how much you like them.

c. Via Nikki Blonsky Cameo.

d. Be a normal decent human.

WHAT TO DO AFTER FIRING SOMEONE

It's not just the firing part; there's a lot more at play. Life goes on once you have dashed their dreams of corporate glory. Here are some tips:

Time It So You Don't See Them in the Parking Lot After

Mama. Mortified. Plucked. Can you imagine? Loading your fine leather computer bag into your new BMW while they sulk away to their old Ford Escort and wonder how they will pay their bills? Or even worse, you slither to your parking space just in time to watch your coworker-until-five-minutes-ago Marjorie let the air out of your tires and write "blood money devil bitch" on the hood of your car with piss? That would be pretty uncomfortable. You'll definitely need a few rounds of mojitos at the Soho House with Kris Jenner to shake it off.

Give Them Severance

It's the least you can do while they search for a new job. Just because they no longer work for you doesn't mean they don't deserve food, water, and moderately good Wi-Fi. Unless they're getting fired for something disgusting like sexual assault or being racist. Then you should drive to their house and burn it down. As you roast a marshmallow over the corpses of the former employee's children, you can browse Indeed for qualified candidates.

Remember That It's Just Business, Baby

It might seem like you are snuffing out someone's life, but it's just their livelihood. And only their *current* livelihood. They might walk into a job they are much better suited for or maybe even something they suck at but truly enjoy. Maybe they'll start making slimes on Etsy or selling LuLaRoe leggings (see Katya's chapter "Scams"). Or maybe they'll be selected to compete in a reality TV competition about drag and end up writing a book about work in eight years.

QUITTING

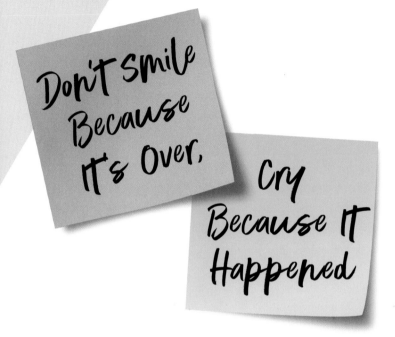

Don't smile Because It's Over,

Cry Because It Happened

BY KATYA

My favorite part about any job is the end. So much of workplace fantasy revolves around the many ways we can bring all the suffering to a screeching halt and release ourselves from the soul-crushing burden of the contemporary dungeon known as work. The only way we are able to endure pain is by holding on to the knowledge that it will someday end. We fantasize about the day when this will all be over. What will we do? What will our face look like with a smile spread across it? What greatness will we accomplish with the new brain space we have once we've evicted all work thoughts? There are so many more sensory elements that could be Pavlovian triggers of pleasure. The sound of dragging our work files into the computer trash bin, the scent of dumping our polyester contempo-casual

work clothes into the actual trash bin, and the feeling of clicking the decline button on an incoming work call.

Monday morning. The alarm clock goes off at 6:00 a.m. You scrape yourself off the bed, internally screaming, and throw yourself into the shower. After choking down three cups of coffee and a dry piece of toast, you shuffle into the car and enter the gridlock on the freeway to make it on time to your thankless, shitty job. And as you glance at the clock to see how late you're going to be, it occurs to you that last Friday you quit.

Suddenly, the world lights up like a divine lotus, glittering in the sacred rays of sunshine. So, you swerve over four lanes of traffic and take the nearest exit and google the directions to the nearest trampoline facility. You change into some dirty workout clothes from your trunk and bounce away with the suburban cheerleader squad for six hours until you pass out. You come to as a twenty-year-old trampoline park employee dangles smelling salts over your face. He says, "Hey, there you are," and you laugh. You both are laughing now. Is it the lack of oxygen to your brain, or is he kind of cute? He writes his number on the back of your receipt, and you go on a date, and another date, and another one, until you eventually move in together, and then he proposes to you at the same trampoline park where you first met, and then you get married in a gorgeous Roman Catholic ceremony, and have a beautiful, aerodynamic family. If you hadn't quit your job on that fateful Friday, you would still be there right now, letting your perky breasts and ass slowly wilt in the stale office air under the harsh corporate overhead lighting.

Even in the rare circumstance where you don't get swept up in a movie romance as a direct result of quitting, there is still a cathartic joy in freeing yourself from the job that had its stiletto heel on your neck for the past eighteen months. That's why I am a strong proponent of Quitting, Quitting Hard, and Quitting NOW.

Quitting often gets a really bad rap. In our fast-paced, achievement-oriented, ambition-obsessed environment, quitting seems like the ultimate act of giving up, a humiliating surrender leaving you labeled a loser. In late capitalism, the ideal worker is applauded for selfless acts of overachievement, an ideology fueled by the belief that work is its own reward and that endless toil is the pathway to a far-off promise of salvation in the form of retirement. However, I feel like you shouldn't put yourself in the direct line of suffering and abuse, especially in exchange for an underwhelming benefits package. Apparently that's controversial? But I will be brave enough to say it: If your job is making you feel bad, and you want to quit, do it. Especially if you have the savings to do it! Nobody's on their deathbed saying, "I wish I hadn't quit that job. I wish I had had the courage to endure five to ten more years of suffering and fruitless toiling so that impatient consumers could receive their useless goods at an unnecessarily breakneck speed."

If you're on the fence about whether to pull the plug on this lifeless job, here are a few points to consider:

- Weigh the pros and cons of staying and leaving. Do you rely on this job for insurance? Would you have to get your own coverage, or finally marry your flop boyfriend to get on his plan? The internet is not a great primary care provider. Healthcare is an important issue. But, on the other side, if your job is creating health problems for you, like night terrors and stress-related rashes that bloom across your arms every time your boss's number shows up on your phone, it's time to take your health into your own hands.

- While you have your thinking cap on (hey, you look great in hats, by the way! you should wear them more often), it's not a bad idea to itemize your monthly expenses to see exactly how much money you have to bring in every month to stay afloat. Can you trim the fat at all? Have you been spending an extraordinary amount of money on fine Italian meats that you could bear to go without? While I agree that prosciutto tastes great with Ma's gravy, I'm just trying to let you know about one of many ways you can set yourself up for success in your new life once you leave your current job.

So, I take it you're ready to quit. Great! Now it's time to figure out your course of action. It's time to submit a letter of resignation to let your employer know you're hitting the road. That's why I generously prepared this foolproof sample. This message would look fabulous printed on creamy card stock in rich, heavy black ink, but just as nice scrawled with a stubby crayon on the back of a takeout menu.

Dear _____,

Please accept this letter as notice of my resignation from this position, effective immediately. I wish I could say that I had received an offer for a more lucrative position at an even more profitable company, but this is not the case. In fact, I have no plan whatsoever going forward, but the pain I am experiencing has left me no choice but to leave quietly and calmly. Otherwise, you and everyone else in this building will have to witness a horror whose aftershocks will reverberate throughout these rancid hallways for generations to come.

I cannot continue to breathe in the clinical, sauerkraut-tinged air of the office once more to repossess my belongings, so please give my desk tchotchkes to _____ from the _____ department, for she is the only individual employed by this company who has even half a soul.

I would like to thank you for this opportunity, as I have come to know a despair so hellish and so frightening that whatever misfortunes I may encounter in the future will pale in comparison to the excruciating hell that I have endured here.

Sincerely,

_____

In the event that your employer does not even deserve the recognition of the preceding letter, I have also prepared a short-form version to be slipped under the door or written on the mirror of the ladies' room in lipstick. Sometimes, less is more.

Short version:

To whom it may concern:

Eat shit and die,

Love,
Bonnie

When Quitting Day finally rolls around, make sure to wear a great outfit, especially one that makes your butt look fabulous, so they always have that memory of you walking away like a bad bitch. Your bodacious figure will be branded onto their brains forever: the indelible image of your confident, big-butted silhouette sashaying out the door of that flop company and bouncing on to bigger and brighter opportunities, just you and your beautiful huge big fat butt.

They say when one door closes, another opens. But sometimes it's best to jump out the window. And when you're free on a Tuesday at 11:00 a.m. while all your friends are trapped at the office, you can thank me.

GETTING FIRED

Need Help Packing?

BY TRIXIE

First things first: I would say most people have been fired but they just don't talk about it. One of the personas to take on when fired is that of a battle-worn castoff who was just dumped by your boyfriend, Corporation A. The other option is far less flattering: to be an absolute off-the-rails Bitter Betty. "That place is being run by idiots! They didn't fire me—I QUIT!" Your left eye twitches as you try to convince everyone in the room, including yourself, that you were wrongfully terminated. But unless your name is Sarah Connor, I have found that most termination is fairly placed in the universe.

Life is full of many experiences that feel nothing like the TV version of the moment when you are living it in real time. Being fired is not one of those experiences. Being fired feels like a faithful shot-for-shot remake of every firing scene in a movie. A moment of disbelief, a beat of shame, and then glares of reproach as you are escorted out of the building with your cardboard box of desk toys and a potted succulent. You sit on the curb in your Christopher & Banks pencil skirt and Fashion Bug blouse and scroll Twitter while you wait for your boyfriend to pick you up. It begins to rain. You realize you don't have a boyfriend. You Uber home, resubscribe to Indeed, and begin the whole process anew.

Why do I have such a vivid recollection of being "let go"? Because I, Tracy Martel, have been fired four separate times. Pretty much the only job I haven't been fired from is this one, and that's because I'm self-employed. I am my own boss! My very own Michael Scott. I am, however, disappointed in the performance of my primary employee—specifically in the "first draft of book deadline" department.

I will now walk you through every job I've ever been fired from. I'll try not to paint myself as a terrible employee, but if at any moment in the next section you feel like Catherine Zeta-Jones doing a full "Cell Block Tango (He Had It Comin')" chair performance, please remember that I go through life as either an idiot who means well or a genius who doesn't care what happens next. I have no flattering middling state.

Stogie Hut on Downer Avenue

Now, this is an employment opportunity that truly gave me a Tarantino-style glimpse into my future firing before it even began. I was eighteen years old, and I had just arrived at the University of Wisconsin–Milwaukee. My roommate, who loved gold chains, aggressive rap music, and fighting with his girlfriend, Claudia, had just dropped out and I needed a job. I took the GreenLine bus route to Downer Avenue in Milwaukee, a jaunty avenue of independent restaurants, vintage clothing stores, and beauty parlors.

As I ambled south, I came upon a store where an employee was being physically thrown out of the building. A firing was occurring in real time! A seven-foot-tall man named Little Shrimpy was screaming out the front door of Stogie Hut: "Don't ever come back, you little bitch!" The freshly fired employee truly ran away down the street. Little Shrimpy stood on the stoop and cussed some more about the unsatisfactory employee and wondered aloud, "Where will I find someone on

short notice?" Enter Brian Firkus: a new freshman wearing all corduroy and flannel with a bandana around my head (I was dating a guy in a band, so I was going through a hipster phase) holding a freshly printed résumé. After a verbal interview that lasted about ninety seconds and only briefly investigated whether I knew what a cigar was, I was brought inside and immediately began a crash course in cigars.

To this day, I know nothing about cigars. They are expensive, smelly, and somehow kind of sad-looking to me. It's never a confident, nice man smoking a cigar. Rather, a cigar is an efficient means of signaling that you have a small dick and you want to look like a cartoon villain. The only culturally acceptable cigar in my opinion should be immediately following the delivery of a baby, and even then, it should happen immediately following the birth—if not during.

I never learned about cigars. I made no effort to absorb or retain any information surrounding this disgusting phenomenon. I distinctly remember someone perusing the humidor and fishing for a recommendation. He asked me what a cigar tasted like. "Smoky," I replied, and went back to my Math 106 homework. However, what I lacked in information I made up for in fabulous salesmanship. I sold a lot of cigars without any actual knowledge of the product. I have a knack for selling things. I could sell shampoo to a bald person. I could sell an unwashed dick to a Kinsey 6 lesbian. I even sold a book to you, the reader, and you're fatally illiterate.

My firing was overdue but not surprising. The owner left a voicemail on the store phone instructing Little Shrimpy to "let that faggot go." I had left a potted plant out overnight and the bitter Milwaukee autumn had frozen and killed it. I felt I gave an above-average effort at the job considering I was eighteen and getting paid near minimum wage, but alas. I was tired of keeping my cigar-smelling clothes in garbage bags under my dorm bed anyway. I was also masturbated in front of at this job, but I have come to understand as a comedienne that being sexually assaulted at work is an early mark of success.

CommTell

I'll say that in this case the firing was a less bizarre feeling than the actual work itself. During my undergraduate degree, I was truly struggling financially. I couldn't even use an ATM because they dispensed bills in twenty-dollar increments and, Mary, I didn't have it. I responded to an on-campus call-to-action for a job posting that advertised "flexible pay, paid training, and a fast-paced environment."

What I got was a job at CommTell, a giant blue office building downtown where I would punch in, plug a headset into a computer, and caption phone calls for the deaf. CommTell basically provides a service where people who have difficulty hearing can use a landline phone more easily. For thirty hours a week, I would get paid nine dollars an hour to eavesdrop on the deaf and their loved ones in order to provide transcribed captioning for the call.

While the job was extremely easy, CommTell wanted absolute attention given by the employees to the audio being transcribed. Between my fast typing skills and my excellent revoicing into the headset, I could truly do the job in my sleep. And I often did nod off, but that's not why I was fired.

It was a snowy December in Milwaukee, and I had been invited to an ugly-sweater Christmas party. In an effort to truly gag the children at the house party, I had sourced puff paint, glitter, and sequins. Because of a time crunch, I decided to bring my couture project to work (time theft hadn't been invented by Jeff Bezos yet) and finish it on the clock. I was embellishing a sweater within an inch of its life. Between phrases I'd glue, stitch, and otherwise adorn. Multitasking, America! Frankly, I should have been given a raise for my tactful use of excess company time.

Mid-sequin, my supervisor, Asha, unplugged my headset and escorted me to the HR department. It was there that CommTell coached me to resign from my post in exchange for a positive reference on my résumé. I didn't know at the time that I was being opted into a resignation so that the company wouldn't owe me an unemployment package. The trickery! The story came to a yuletide close when I emerged at the holiday hootenanny crying, broke, but positively chic—and being admired by your peers is a more robust form of sustenance than unemployment.

MAC Cosmetics

Before I strut down this runway of my memory, let me say that every person who is influential and chic has at one point worked at and been fired from MAC Cosmetics.

I was with MAC for almost five years when the hammer came down on my young gay life. MAC was the first time I was truly all in at a job; I honestly believe doing makeup at the mall was my calling. Starting at sixteen dollars an hour, I was the richest of my friends, and my makeup addiction was *fed*, honey.

One day I went into work and was stopped upon punching in. I was called in to loss prevention at the mall and fully interrogated. I was viciously accused of stealing product from the store, and despite my pleading truths, I was dismissed and suspended from work. I got a call two days later from the regional manager, who let me know I was officially "terminated." I hung up, dropped my phone, and proceeded to sob for days. Looking back, I think I overreacted. But I was stunned—I was so good at my job and so invested in my growth at the company that I never saw a firing coming. My integrity and self-image were very tied up in my work ethic and my place at MAC, so it was a really hard thing to not ugly-cry through.

However, I had to look in the dressing-room mirror and take some responsibility for what was next. I decided to use the time available to me to double my drag show bookings and film an audition tape for a TV show called *RuPaul's Drag Race*. I have often wondered: If I hadn't been fired, would I have auditioned? Probably not. The process is notoriously arduous—not to mention I had to save up money for a camera and then teach myself Final Cut to complete the submission.

Now, instead of selling blot powder at the mall, I'm selling books to people like you. Without the magic of firing, you wouldn't even be reading this; you'd be stumbling through some kind of *12 Rules to Being a Fierce Diva* coffee table book written by Meghan McCain's makeup artist.

It's important to recognize that there are two types of people: those who have been fired and those who haven't been fired *yet*. When it happens to you, I recommend you cling to your dignity like whoa, save your money, and refocus. Maybe you start a YouTube channel where you decorate cupcakes; maybe you do an Etsy selling Jesse Eisenberg jewelry. But the universe is a snappy gay stage manager and it's important to listen to her shrill and mysterious commands.

PASSION PROJECTS

From The Hobby to The Lobby

BY KATYA

At this point, dear reader, it's quite possible you may be seized by the dull ache of boredom with all this dreary office talk and nine-to-five jibber-jabber. How do you think I feel? I've had to write so much of it, and deep down I'm a card-carrying commie to the core, or at least I was in a not-so-distant past life. I think it's time to ditch this tepid water cooler mumbo jumbo in favor of some eye-watering, bowel-destroying extra-spicy alternative-lifestyle gumbo. And can you guess what the secret ingredient is in this exotic signature stew? It's passion.

For many people, the things you love may be located outside the office, and that's okay. There is an unfortunate tendency for an obsessive hobby or passionate pursuit to lose its luster, and that's just common sense if you think about it.

One of the reasons a hobby is so enjoyable is because it exists outside the constraints of time and pressure—it's the respite from that state of mind. That being said, if given the chance to work full-time in the New York Philharmonic Orchestra rather than haul bricks down at the quarry, I'm quite sure Young Timmy the French horn player will happily choose the former. Still, if you do anything for a long time, it can become dull. This is the nature of things. That's how rocks get so fucking smooth, which I just learned about yesterday, and I still can't believe it. Those ocean waves just beat the shit out of those rocks little by little, day by day, until you're walking along the shore and the perfect-size stone, smooth as a baby's ass, is waiting for you to pick it up and chuck it at the seagull that pecked out your nephew Timmy's left eye.

And after a trip to the emergency room, several rounds of radiation, and expensive physical therapy, what is Timmy left with, other than a snazzy eye patch? A more finely tuned set of ears, perfect for giving him that extra edge he

needs in order to get into Juilliard. See, things have a way of working out in the end. Or they don't, but it's all part of the universe's plan for you. And if I know one thing about the universe, it's that she is out there, with big boobs, a paint-brush, and a plan meticulously designed just for you.

For as long as I can remember, I have been deeply enthralled by and totally envel-oped in a variety of interests and activities to a religious level of ecstasy. When I was eleven years old, I discovered Cirque du Soleil and decided with unflappable preteen conviction that I would become a circus performer. Alone and gay in the suburbs with no circus coach to guide me, I began a rigorous self-directed train-ing program, which consisted of tumbling on the trampoline in the backyard, followed by unsupervised sessions of extreme backbending. I would watch and rewatch VHS copies of contortionist acts and then just jam my gay little body into these shapes until one day I was able to lie prone, flip my legs over my head, and straighten them out in front of me. It is difficult for me to describe the mix-ture of pain, joy, fear, and wonder that occurs when you feel your ass press gently into the crown of your head. I suppose you could call it passion.

I remained steadfast in my determination to fulfill my life's passion, and so I had my whole life mapped out. I would skip college and enroll in the Montréal Circus School in Québec, and then I would subsequently be drafted into Cirque du Soleil. This was not only the plan, it was my destiny, and there was nothing you could say to my grotesquely bending fourteen-year-old self that would convince me otherwise.

Until I found satanism. Then that was my passion. It's not that contortion and satanism are incompatible—most acrobats do worship the devil, and all of them are gay—but those passionate pursuits are often fueled by fickle flames, and there's no telling where the wind will blow. Foreign language study soon eclipsed the dark arts, then yoga, then drugs (which is more of a lifestyle and less of a hobby), and then drag, and so on.

There is a persistent mythology about pursuing one's passion, an idealized vision of work filled with meaning, purpose, and joy. This is frequently referred to as a calling, especially by those who are drawn to the clergy or service work.

I know people who believe they have heard the voice of God literally call them to action, and while some of those people were on the tail end of a meth binge, others soberly found that purposeful path.

"Do something you love, and you'll never work a day in your life." I heard this expression a lot growing up, and I could never quite pinpoint why I found it unsettling, but now I realize it's because it was probably uttered by someone very rich and permanently out to lunch. To quote a *Drag Race* alumna: "What privilege." When it comes to choosing a line of work that is so interesting and suited to your abilities and enjoyable that it feels like you shouldn't be getting paid for it . . . well, good luck. To quote her again: "What you *wanna* do is not necessarily what you're *gonna* do." And that can be a hard pill to swallow.

I went to art school to pursue the most lucrative career path I could think of: performance art. For four years, I lived in an insulated bubble of my own artistic fantasies, completely untethered from any practical earthly concerns. No thought was given to making or saving money, how to plan for the future, or even what would occur the day after graduation. I was too busy videotaping myself scarfing down a mountain of doughnuts or mapping out durational performance pieces where I would hump a wall for four hours.

Looking back, it's actually quite impressive how absorbed and focused, and blissfully free from anxiety about the future, I was able to be. Then, a few months before graduation, I slowly started to visualize what lay ahead on the horizon: It was hazy at first, but as each day passed it became more and more clear: the looming threat of abject poverty. So I skipped graduation to go camping in the pouring rain of Scotland, where I was able to sample the wet and wild flavors of homelessness.

When I returned from the West Highland Way hiking trip, I was promptly bitch-slapped with the icy-cold claw of reality. I was broke, and I had no marketable skills, no car, and certainly no plan. So I went to live with my parents and applied to work at a bookstore down the street, close enough for me to commute on my bicycle. I'll never forget the manager opening the interview with, "Just so you know, the pay is only seven dollars an hour," and it was clear that many people took that as their cue to exit politely and find something more dignified. Well, I had no dignity, so I took the job, an inventory shift from 6:00 a.m. to 2:00 p.m. every day working alongside a fifty-year-old Dungeons & Dragons enthusiast and a cheerful Chinese woman whose smile was grotesquely streaked every other day by bleeding gums.

I worked there for six months and fantasized about suicide every night. I eventually saved enough money to move back to the city, renting a closet-size room in a dilapidated five-bedroom house with a rodent-infested daycare on the first floor. The rent was $250 a month; included in that bargain was a five-hour-a-month commitment of hard labor around the house, plus daily tending of the wood-burning fireplace that provided the only source of heat to the illegal stone hut that housed the landlady out back.

Eventually, through a friend from school, I got hooked up with my first drag gig, and thus began my passionate love affair with the art of being a professional drag queen. This was absolutely nowhere on my childhood destiny road map, but life has a way of providing you with opportunities that you can handle, especially if you're a white man. And for this white man, deciding to be a fake Russian woman was my holy grail. When *Drag Race* started airing on television, I watched it with wide eyes and gritted teeth, like many of my nonfamous colleagues, thinking, "Well, I can do that." After its second season, when a local queen by the name of Jujubee received her golden ticket, I began submitting my own audition tapes in earnest. I received a callback for season three and, like any excited dummy, chose to interpret that as undeniable proof that I would be cast. I waited patiently by the phone for days that stretched into weeks, reassuring myself with any number of wild justifications as to why they hadn't called. Eventually, soaked in the steamy funk of rejection like a lonely, acne-ridden teenager waiting by the window in her prom dress two months after the school year has ended, I unplugged the phone, hung up my strapless gown, and came to terms with the reality—I wouldn't be going to the big dance this year, but at least I wouldn't have to burn down the entire gym with everyone in it.

Of course, as Madonna so creepily whispers in her 1994 song "Forbidden Love," "rejection is the greatest aphrodisiac." So I submitted another audition tape, and another, followed by yet another. Many people who seek to make a living doing something they love, especially in the field of art and entertainment, will likely find themselves at this desolate place. It's the fork in the road where your passion is pitted against your patience and your pocketbook: Should I keep trying? Can I afford to keep going? Is it even worth it? Or should I just resign myself to something that seems a lot duller but also much more stable?

I was fortunate enough to be one of the lucky ones who got to have their "big break," although at the time I wasn't so sure that's what was going on. I had decided to ease out of performing and had already begun preparing to apply to graduate school to become a social worker. This is a well-trodden path for many people in recovery who are motivated for a second act. I was taking courses at a community college to fill in some credit gaps from my wildly unuseful bachelor of fine arts degree when the casting people for *Drag Race* rang me up. They were wondering if I had planned on submitting an audition video that year. The truth was, I hadn't, as I felt that the previous year's tape was the best I could do, and my attitude was something like the old Porkchop adage: "If they want me, they want me; if they don't, they don't." The phone call, however, seemed to indicate that perhaps they did in fact want me, but the casting agent wouldn't give me a straight answer when I asked her. All she said was that if I was interested in being on the show, I should do another tape. Again, always one to put the cart before the horse, I chose to interpret this as a guarantee that I would be cast, but this time, I would learn several weeks later, I was right.

Getting on *Drag Race* turned out to be quite the game changer for me, just like it had been for Juju. In just a few years I got the chance to accomplish way more than I would have imagined I'd be capable of doing in an entire lifetime. And I got to experience the highlights of my earlier dreams and ambitions without any of their downsides. I could incorporate my love of painting and drawing as little or as much as I wanted to, I could do the same with my fondness for foreign languages, and I could feel like a contortionist onstage without having to undergo the rigorous training or endure the crippling back pain that inevitably haunts every circus performer.

One of the problems that I would eventually discover with becoming successful at expressing yourself is that the business of being you becomes an operation that must be run by more people than just you. I was the little girl who dreamed of making muffins, then one day discovered that people were interested in eating my muffins. And before I knew it, I had a bakery, and hired several bakers to help me meet the demand for muffins. But eventually my passion for making muffins began to fade, even as the muffin business boomed, until one night I accidentally burned down the bakery.

What's the point of that muffin story? I suppose it's a cautionary tale for those of you lucky enough to achieve overnight success in a field you are passionate about, so that you don't get carried away and overwhelmed to the point where you can't tell the difference between a delicious homemade muffin and a high-heeled shoe. You might end up naked and disoriented in the middle of the street, where your landlord finds you at 3:00 a.m. gnawing on a shoe, with your feet covered in muffins.

13 REASONS WHY
(NOT TO BE A DRAG QUEEN)

BY TRIXIE

At eighteen I started cross-dressing for money. Well, to be honest, I didn't start cross-dressing for money 'til about three years into it. The first few years were entirely out of pocket. A true moneysuck that was never intended to be fruitful, lucrative, or even something I would continue doing for any foreseeable future. Through fifteen years of carrying suitcases, shaving my back, and physically fighting bachelorettes, I have accidentally risen to the top 0.0000000001 percent of drag queen success stories. I have achieved more than my wildest dreams and made more money than I knew one person could without selling drugs or even killing someone.

Now, by basically shitting on every single career option by way of "keeping it real" with you, Katya and I may have actually talked you off the ledge of many different types of jobs through the journey of this book. And that's good. My only fear here would be that we might have accidentally nudged you *on*to the ledge of the worst career of all—drag. Because this is a book penned by two successful cross-dressers, you have begun to see yourself among our ranks and part of an exciting new career venture involving wigs, sequins, and pretending to sing other people's music. You may have even become so deluded that you find my situations as Trixie appealing or even inspirational.

My story is not one of inspiration. It is a remote fluke that is peppered with downsides. I want to let you, the reader, know that drag is not a get-rich-quick scheme and it will quickly overstay its welcome in your life like an unwanted houseguest, taking up space and spending your money. Read ahead for some cleanly organized points of interest on the road to cross-dressing hell.

1. **Late nights.** Yes, we all like to party, Mama. But when you are doing a full Lady Gaga "club, 'nother club, 'nother club, plane, NO SLEEP" lifestyle Thursday through Sunday on a weekly basis, your biological clock can altogether lose its regularity. You become a fabled specter from the hours of 5:00 a.m. to 2:00 p.m., and it is impossible to rouse yourself, let alone keep a professional or social engagement. You rot on the vine, and the process is nearly irreversible.

2. **Early mornings.** This is what they don't tell you about being a drag queen. In the beginning, the aforementioned late nights are your bread and butter—too many of them, but consistently late. You wake up at 3:00 p.m., buy an iced coffee the size of God, hot-glue drag for a few hours while live-tweeting some piece of reality television, and then start painting and drinking by 7:00 p.m. What they don't tell you is that if you are lucky enough to come upon dollops of success in this field, they put you in front of something called a camera. Cameramen, sound technicians, and directors all notoriously have children, wives, and many other pointless attachments. And they like a workday to end squarely at 5:00 p.m., which means you, the cross-dresser,

are tasked with being showered, shaved, and stage-ready often before 10:00 a.m. Empathy for the nocturnal nature of drag is not present on the call sheet of life, so greeting the morning with cheap perfume and stacked wigs becomes a sad and regular occurrence.

3. **A young person's game.** If you were in any other job, at thirty you'd be an ambitious and bright young thing often trying to skew older with your looks in an effort to "get this bread." In drag, you are geriatric by the age of thirty. A majority of drag queens start at twenty-one years old, and most have the common sense to bow out while the gig is still cute. By your thirties you are performing music that the twenty-one-year-olds have never heard of. Your fashion references are tired, and you are considered "old-school" because you still wear a bra, corset, and padding to the drag show.

4. **No pay.** It's rather humorous to me that nowadays homosexuals will buy one (1) wig on Amazon, procure one (1) booking, and immediately resign from their 401(k)-with-full-benefits day job. Having a "real" job is a sign of weakness, and only cross-dressers who have fully shaved off their eyebrows are considered to be taking it seriously. Because of television, new drag queens see drag as a get-rich-quick scheme with a yellow brick road that leads straight from the gay bars to the bank. Nothing could be further from the truth. No exaggeration: 99 percent of drag queens do not live off drag as a job. It's typically fruitless labor, and the best you can hope for is to pay for drinks and the Uber home.

5. **High probability of sexual misconduct.** Hi, are you doing drag? Well then, buckle up, because you're about to get fingered against your will by a bridesmaid. Or you're about to be cornered and

accosted by a transamorous bouncer. Or you're about to have a teen girl read erotic fan fiction to you against your will at DragCon. Or you're about to be flashed by an Uber driver who just wants you to know how beautiful you are and also can he come up to your apartment and use the bathroom? I often feel like I am performing a stream-of-consciousness improv version of the movie *Monster*, where I am Charlize Theron if she didn't gain the weight for the role. If you choose drag as your main gig, get ready to duct tape your hole closed regularly because the Lyft driver is absolutely trying to fuck you on the way to the gig, and once you're there, a straight woman in a blue wig at a gay bar is going to lick your face on her Snapchat.

6. **Never be attractive to men again.** If you have ever for a moment caught yourself in a mirror and believed that you possess any attractiveness to offer the world, then I hope you are ready for that chapter of your life to be over. The facts are very simple, folks. Gay men are not attracted to men who do drag. Even those of us who still have eyebrows and mild fitness are invisible to other gay men. Admittedly, due to the popularity of televised drag shows, the situation is slowly improving. Now if you're a TV drag queen, a guy might fuck you only to reveal later that he collects drag queen loads like Pokémon cards. Your options are to slither into a box under your bed and denounce your genitals or begin the search for some unfathomable unicorn who can stay hard in you knowing that you lip sync with a wig on for a living. Good luck.

7. **Takes up too much space.** The average gay man owns 350 floral button-ups, 275 V-necks, 56 pairs of skinny jeans, 210 snapback hats, and 195 pairs of overpriced sneakers. A gay man's closet overrunneth with a decade of embarrassing clothes spanning from Hollister to Old Navy to Target's Pride Month offerings.

There is room for improvement, but no room for clothing. Now imagine stacking an entire other fake person's wardrobe on top of that in your closet. I personally own more than 100 wigs, hundreds of dresses, 50-plus pairs of women's shoes, and hundreds of pieces of jewelry. I live in a three-bedroom condo that my boyfriend can't even move into because he would have to set up his home office literally inside the oven. Drag is like heroin in that it slowly takes everything away from you, starting with your dignity but ending with closet space.

8. **Packing suitcases.** I live in a *Groundhog Day* scenario involving packing and unpacking suitcases. I spend more time packing up costumes and wigs and makeup than I do actually onstage or on camera. It's impossible to come home blackout drunk and unpack a suitcase. But if you let your musty costumes rot in a suitcase for too long, you open up the luggage a few days later and find a fragrant loaf of sourdough baking inside.

9. **Uber drama.** This concept is very simple: Ubering in drag is weird. Best-case scenario, you are ignored but the driver radiates hate. Worst-case scenario, the driver slows down, sees you, and immediately cancels the ride right in front of your salad. The typical scenario involves the aforementioned sexual assault.

10. **Everyone thinks you know where to get drugs.** Now, for some of you who deal drugs, I would imagine this might be kind of nice—lucrative, even. As a drag queen, you are the life of the party, but you are also expected to be the operator who connects individuals to the pharmacist of the party. I'm sure that for a normal drag queen, that perceived edginess might be ideal, but for those of us who are a bizarre cross between a Powerpuff Girl and Mrs. Doubtfire, it's a constant branding issue.

11. **Physical pain.** If you would like to know what it's like to give birth to a watermelon filled with razor blades, do drag. If you want to know what it's like to be hobbled by Kathy Bates à la *Misery* while the *Jigsaw* reverse bear trap helmet goes off, do drag. If you want to have your actual nail beds ache on a Sunday morning, do drag.

12. **Immigration.** Your life as a human traveler is about to get very complicated. Not only do you have a fake job that puzzles every immigration agent. Not only do you have no eyebrows and a neon yellow bowl cut as your boy drag. You look suspicious because you ARE suspicious. You are basically traveling with disguises, cash, and a passport book with stamps from every country that allows gays in.

13. **Meghan McCain DMs you.**

ILLICIT PROFESSIONS

Doing Business in The Shadows

BY KATYA

If you've left your job and are thinking of new ways to get back in the moneymaking game, there are many wonderful career options you might not have yet considered. The reality is that many legitimate forms of moneymaking are unethical, and vice versa. Sometimes, the difference between a drug dealer and a psychiatrist is a piece of paper. There are illegal drug dealers who pay more attention to their clients' needs and histories than actual Beverly Hills doctors who charge two hundred dollars for every fifteen minutes. And drug dealers often have more legible penmanship.

The sex work industry consists of a vast and varied landscape, but the average person rarely gets an accurate picture of the true lived experience of a pavement-pounding insider. When we think of hookers, we conjure images of Julia Roberts in a crop top and miniskirt nervously strolling Rodeo Drive, or a nameless corpse in

cheap heels peeking out of a bathroom stall in a crime franchise (hi, Willam). Prostitution is a crime in most places, so our perception of those who sell sex for money is distorted through the shitty blue lens of law enforcement. But there is a sunnier side to red-light labor, and I am fortunate enough to have had some great and very enriching experiences, both personally and financially, hawking my puss.

Like any job, sex work offers a wide range of earning potential. At the top, you have your ultra-high-priced escort, flown out to Dubai to entertain some Saudi royal, who could rake in a hundred thousand dollars in a weekend. On the other side of the spectrum, you'll find the more recognizable set of less financially stable streetwalking hos. The first distinction to make here: Are we strutting for twenty bucks and an 8 ball in the moonlight, or are we a self-sufficient full-time work-from-home kind of gal?

I personally fell somewhere in the middle of the spectrum: While it was never my full-time job, there were a few years when I met up with paying customers anywhere from two to six times a month and could bring home anywhere from one hundred to five hundred dollars each time.

Now, keep in mind, this was way before the advent of OnlyFans, webcamming, and the plethora of digital outlets where you can monetize your sexuality by self-producing erotic content at your own pace and on your own terms.

My first shift as a freelance hooker happened by accident, and thankfully not the kind of accident involving chloroform, the trunk of a car, and then being chained to a radiator in the basement of a restaurant. For years, I lived above a gay bar in Boston that featured drag show entertainment every night of the week, and was also a discreet hangout for trans women, cross-dressers, and their admirers. Some of the girls were there on business, others just to live their feminine fantasy, and I was mostly naive enough to not be able to tell the difference.

One Wednesday night I was there in drag, performing in a show with an audience of zero people, so I wiggled over to the other side of the bar, where there was some action. I crossed paths with a man who was basically a stock photo of a businessman: Bob Regular from Office #1.

The most interesting thing I observed in these spaces was that most of the time, if a man was interested, he would let you know in the most direct, no-nonsense, unambiguous language, as if he were on a speed-dating show and if he didn't pick up a hooker in twenty seconds he would be pummeled with a cartoon hammer.

So Bob Regular spotted me, his eyes widened (I looked stunning), and he marched directly over to me with all the confidence of a forty-five-year-old white middle manager. He stopped about three inches from my face to tell me I was beautiful and that he would love to spend some time with me right then. He wasn't ugly, so it was a perfect match; I decided to bring him up to my apartment. He sat on my couch and told me he would love to see me do a dance, and he would really love to see me smoke. I draw the line at dancing, but then I hop right over it for smoking, so we had a deal.

I started to slither and sway in a kind of old-fashioned carnival peep show snake-lady dance in my extremely dark, single-votive-candlelit apartment and sexily smoked a cigarette. Then, apparently so enthralled by my alluring display, he started jerking off. As I sensually strutted over to lend him a hand, I caught a hazy glimpse of something suspicious. It was hard to discern in the near pitch darkness of my boudoir, but as I approached in slow erotic motion, my cataracts adjusted enough to recognize that this man had some kind of sexually transmitted situation unfolding all around his between-me-down-there.

I did a graceful pivot away, pas de bourrée, and sashayed back to my little peep-show perch and ratcheted up the sexy on my undulating choreo so that he could get his nut as soon as possible. Eventually, he came, thank God, zipped up, and I, thoroughly disappointed, politely showed him to the door. Once he was gone, I turned the lights on, slumped down on the other cushion of the couch, and lit a cigarette. As I heaved a dramatic sigh of dejection, I happened to notice something stuck between the cushions. Was that . . . money? Yes, it certainly was. Two crisp twenty-dollar bills, left discreetly by Mr. Spotted Dick himself.

If my bathroom had a tub, this would have been my cue to frolic around in a bubble bath listening to Prince's "Kiss," for this was my *Pretty Woman* moment. It was official: I had accidentally found my new purpose, my calling.

And although this was definitely not the Regent Beverly Wilshire, the call did come from inside the house—my house. Before you scoff or snicker at the meager forty-dollar payload, I'd like to remind you that it would have taken me more than five hours of stocking books with my Good Ole Bloody-Gummed Coworker to earn less than I did in twenty minutes. Girlboss.

There are several other important details to acknowledge about the industry. Do you have agency? If your commute to work happens to take place on a shipping container on its way to Greece, the answer is probably no. It's best to get yourself in a position where you can act on your free will and pursue your desire without the involvement of pimps. If you can do that, this job can really be one where you are your own boss. And once you separate yourself from any shame or taboo that society places on this line of work, you can focus on the real issue: staying safe.

Katya's Tips for Sex Work Success

- **No outcalls:** Don't travel to a neighboring village. Keep it at home. It's so much easier when you know where the knives are. If you're a company of one, you've gotta be your own HR and OSHA.

- **Set boundaries:** If you stand for nothing, you'll fall for anything. For me, this meant declining drugs that were often offered to me while working. I didn't want to impair my ability to run a profitable business. The tricky thing here is that the client often sees drugs and paid sex as the same thing. They're just trying to let loose and get crunk, turnt, and lit. It's up to you to draw the lines. If they want the allure of doing drugs with you, just pop a baby aspirin and act like you're tripping.

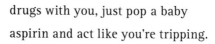

- **Discuss the terms and collect in advance:** What's your rate? Where do you draw the line? One of my best clients was this guy who hated his wife, drove a Beemer, and was very unhappy. I met him at a show and he said, "I'll give you twenty bucks if you rub my shoulders." He kept being like, "Keep going," and handing me more twenties. By the time he handed over a third twenty, it was interrupting the show. *I guess this is a massage parlor now?* I thought. At the end of the show, he approached me outside and said, "Would you like to come to my hotel?" We then proceeded to have the frankest, most efficient discussion of terms. It felt like *Shark Tank*. We were clear on what I was willing to do and what he would pay. We landed on thirty-minute massage, thirty-minute blow job, two hundred bucks. Him: My hotel's around the corner. Me: My apartment's *upstairs*. BAM!

- **Manage your time:** The "make your own schedule" of it all is kind of a fallacy, truth be told. You have to work on the client's timeline. My friend who was a full-timer said that the busiest times for her were the morning and lunchtime, because married men with jobs wanted to get off before walking into the office. I agreed to morning gigs like these a few times, but they were the worst because for a drag queen there are hours of shaving involved. And then sometimes they would cancel, and I would be home and hairless, short of many hours I could have spent doing literally anything else.

- **Create a workable schedule:** To the extent that you *can* control it, give yourself a schedule that is manageable and works for your lifestyle, especially if it's your full-time gig. A friend of mine—a beautiful, lazy friend—had an insatiable sex drive but hated working. At the end of the month when her rent was due, her house turned into the Six Flags of fucking. You would wait in line and she was in there TURNING IT OUT. We met at a bar once during one such end-of-the-month sex marathon and she walked in totally out of breath. "What's wrong?" I asked her. "I just fucked seven guys today. Rent is due tomorrow." Her strategy was a great example of the efficiency that is possible in this industry. Your manipulation of their biology is your new time card. The cock is the new clock.

- **Cultivate hustle, charm, and ingenuity:** If you possess these skills, your ability to make it rain will be limitless. I had a *Pretty Woman* moment myself one time, except the Richard Gere character was a married construction worker who had recently gotten out of prison for marijuana conspiracy. He was so paranoid about herpes (yes, specifically herpes) that he pressured me to get tested constantly. He said he would pay for it to be expedited, which is not a thing. So I did a little creative thinking. I said, "Well, this clinic will do an expedited test, but it will be five hundred dollars to have the results expedited." Since he never asked for a copy of the results, I got an extra five-hundred-dollar supplement to my fee. If he had to cancel, he would pay me a cancellation fee, which he would drop in an empty vase by my bed. If there was an Olympic event for having a great butt and paying hookers well, he would have gotten a gold. He was everything, and he even had the nerve to tell me to my face, "You know, if things were different and people were more accepting, I'd love for you to be my girl." I'm not a girl, but I would've married

him. Seeing him over the course of two to three years of my life was truly the epitome of "Do something you love, and you'll never work a day in your life."

If hooking isn't your gig, but you've got a knack for doing business in the shadows, then you might like to try some of these other underground employment positions:

Mafia Henchperson

This could include everything from filing records and running errands to brutally torturing and killing people. You'll need a strong stomach and a deep sense of loyalty to the cause.

Professional Gambler

If you're a thrill seeker who can't stand being chained to a desk, then this wildly fluctuating position could be for you. The specter of bankruptcy lurks behind every potential jackpot, and the only thing that separates you from just a regular gambler is that you do it all day long!

Drug Dealer

Selling stuff can be really exciting, especially when your product is always in demand. Of course, success in this field can result in an ever-increasing amount of jail time, so it would pay to be cautious and heed the old dealer adage: "Don't get high on your own supply."

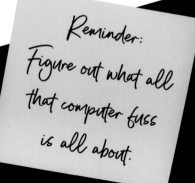

Reminder: Figure out what all that computer fuss is all about.

PROD.

ROLL   SCENE   TAKE

DIRECTOR:

CAMERA:

Date:

Day Nite   Int   Ext   Mos Sync

SHOWBIZ

Entertaintment

BY **TRIXIE**

Your dream job should sometimes stay the job of your dreams. While there are exhilarating careers out there just waiting to be inhabited by mediocre people like you, many career paths catfish as desirable avenues when in fact they are nothing of the sort. They are *old maiden* types of careers. Flight attendant, hairstylist, and bartender are just a few of the vocations that scream "this job is amazing" but truly offer an underhanded whisper of "this job will gut you and carve a smile into your face like a jack-o'-lantern."

Retail is a fabulous example of this. Surface level, the job offers a clean and well-lit work environment, discounts, and the convenience of doing your Hanukkah shopping during your lunch break. After your first eight-hour shift, the honeymoon is over. You've been near lobotomized by the cloying small talk, you were slapped on the clit by a Karen, and you got spit-roasted by the regional manager of operations because you didn't open enough store credit cards to meet quota.

While the retail career catfishing is fierce, there is no bait and switch more stunning than show business. Worst-case scenario, you pound the pavement for decades fruitlessly and are doomed to watch all your dreams come true for people who are thinner and younger than you. Best-case scenario, you catch a lucky break and "make it." You have a right-time-right-place lightning-in-a-bottle scenario that rockets you toward success. But at what cost? Overnight you become transformed into a lunch lady of one-liners slopping the trays of any audience member with a dollar to spend. You end up in Reno crooning your late hit from 1993 while tourists tell you that you look "just like that guy from that thing." Bloated and unfeeling, you chase a bottle of Xanax with one final bubble bath. *Access Hollywood* memorializes you for twelve seconds before snapping back to a story about Apple Paltrow's gender identity and you are never spoken of again.

Some of you reading this chapter have entertainment career goals and are now listlessly scanning the page for guidance. I get asked constantly in interviews, "What advice do you have for people who are just starting drag?" My answer is stalwart and frigid: Get out while you still can. Drag, like show business, was never meant to be a get-rich-quick scheme and should be viewed as more parallel to hard drug use or sex work. How many famous DJs can you think of? One? Five? Now consider how many limp college sophomores are thinking about dropping out to pursue Marshmello dreams.

Success in this industry is atypical. I am an incredible example of success in TV, music, comedy, and many other types of showbiz. However, I am the product of a freak occurrence. I was at a TSA security check completely nude in 1997 when a Wilhelmina Models talent scout bumped into my huge heavy natural breasts in the recombobulation area. After I originally told my story on an episode of *Sally Jessy Raphael*, airports across America flooded with nude women looking to be discovered at a TSA checkpoint. Milwaukee General Mitchell Airport then operated as a brothel for a few weeks before the aspiring models went home with not even a shirt on their backs.

To help you move on from your recently discarded dreams of being a star, I'd like to pitch you several new and exciting career options that people are talking about. Many of these positions are becoming available for you right in your area.

Gravedigger

Now, hear me out: Grave digging is sickening. First, the supply and demand here is an unbreakable chain commonly referred to as "the circle of life." As long as people keep yeeting themselves off bridges or succumbing to old age surrounded by puffy grandchildren, you will always have job security. Also: The upper bodies of gravediggers are notoriously ripped. Nothing sculpts a body quite like disposing of bodies. Plus, when your biological clock starts to wind down and you need a grave dug for yourself, you already know a guy!

Hair Plugs Before-and-After Model

This career might not be ideal for everyone reading this, but for some of you faggy bald fucks, consider this passage your burning bush. For some of you, your gay thirties have crept in through the hairline and you're living in denial. You are that gay person who insists you "have a big forehead" instead of admitting you "have a hairline that has gone the way of *Freaks and Geeks*." It's time to step into the light and, by doing so, let said light refract off your glossed dome and blind an onlooker. You are slipping slowly but not slowly enough into the abyss of old bald gay. If you're any ethnicity besides white, you will complete this transition gracefully and come out the other side even more beautiful to look at. Montel Williams, Vin Diesel, Taye Diggs—all gorgeous and bald. If you're white, you're staring down the barrel of a slippery water slide that shoots you out into the lazy river of grossness. In this river, you are wearing a bucket hat and you have a gratuitous sunburn. You're sixty-five years young, your name is John J. Johnson, and you are telling the poolside teen boys that you used to go to their high school.

BUT there's a way out of this downward spiral. Save up about twenty K, make an appointment, and go get hair plugs. Before the procedure, offer your photos for a before-and-after advertisement in exchange for 10 percent off your procedure. In this scenario, you are technically paying for a service and in no way employed yourself, but you might get recognized at the bodega by another imminent baldy. He'll say, "Aren't you from that thing?" pick up the cost of your coffee, and it will have all been worthwhile.

Bootleg DVD Salesman

This job doesn't seem lucrative, but the number of people selling burned DVDs from the back of a Chevy Corsica would suggest otherwise. As long as there are

Dwayne "The Rock" Johnson films being released on a perennial basis, the bootleg DVD industry will continue to boom. The Fast & Furious franchise alone generates 7.2 billion dollars in bootleg revenue per year. You could get in on the ground floor and all you need is a DVD burner, one original and current hit film, and a great sales pitch. "Would you like to see a movie you don't care about for slightly fewer dollars and cents than the AMC is gouging you for?" Make sure your copies actually play; otherwise, I suggest wigs and accents to eliminate a paper trail.

If these tantalizing enterprises haven't led you away from the flames of showbiz, I guess I can start to coach you on the fundamental avenues in "the biz."

Comedy

Comedy is tough, because I have read the autobiographies of many female comedians and sadly they all tend to take a similar shape. Girl gets traumatized by a family dynamic, girl sees female comedian on public television, girl decides to pursue comedy. Girl bombs for years at every open mic in Manhattan for a decade until she crafts her first solid joke about being sexually assaulted. Ironically, she gets her big break when a senior male comedian masturbates in front of her without her permission. She says nothing for fear of being blacklisted, collects the progressively fatter checks, and someday must process the betrayal onstage in an Emmy-nominated special. She gets sober and moves to Burbank before becoming a lesbian and having an affair with her female ghostwriter. The ghostwriter turns out to be an actual ghost and the story inspires an all-female casting in a remake of *Ghostbusters*. The reviews are mixed.

Singing

There is perhaps a talent no more coveted and fantastic than singing. Opening up your mouth and belting out "The Rose" at karaoke is annoying, but if you can add a little Vaseline on the teeth and some shapewear, a star can be born. Obviously the precursor here is being musically gifted—but honestly not even. Many an elusive chanteuse is not naturally gifted at chanteuse-ing. Luckily with modern technology and some good old-fashioned "watermelon watermelon" lip-syncing, even a complete toad can croak her way to the top of the Billboard charts as long as she has a snatched ponytail and a fat ass. There's a rumor in Hollywood that Dua Lipa is actually just a Roomba in joggers who was discovered playing *Dance Dance Revolution* at Dave & Buster's.

Acting

Any type of talent can surface in any type of person at any time. It's almost random. But a flair for acting is usually only discovered in the deeply mentally ill. Everyone good at acting is either a narcissist or manic depressive. But somehow we revere actors! When your great-aunt Trudy disengages from reality, you put her in a home and cut her nails really short. When Meryl Streep does it, you decorate her in awards and interview her on a red carpet. How many dead rats did Jared Leto have to leave in my dressing room for me to finally say, "I GET IT, YOU'RE A SERIOUS ACTOR!"? The answer is twelve. Stories such as this about prolific actors are rarely tales of how adjusted and normal they are. Great thespians are vibrating on the edge of dissolution at all times, and all they need is a small push to become a twister that picks up their Star Waggons trailer and rockets it across the Hollywood Hills.

Dancing

Apparently dancing is a talent, but let's be honest, folks: Best-case scenario, you get to do a couple barrel rolls in a Doublemint commercial, and then it's curtains on your career, which was make-believe to begin with. However, a dance career isn't without its perks. Dancers generally have incredible physiques and are the most fun people to hit the clubs with. Dancers need about a half sip of vodka before they are doing full jump splits at 2:00 p.m. at the Abbey. Tragically, dancers are usually the most basic people you've ever met in your life. Picture that dumb bitch from your dance team in high school—the one whose profile picture is her doing a stag leap on the beach—and give her a dirty boyfriend. Like white guy with dreadlocks dirty. THAT is a dancer. When I think of dancers, I think of the dance majors at school gathered around a MacBook between classes chewing on almonds and rewatching the movie *Center Stage.*

STAGE NAMES

Now that you've chosen a discipline, we have to decide on a name. After all, a rose by any other name does NOT smell as sweet. William Shakespeare would know: William Shakespeare of Stratford-upon-Avon was his stage name. ("Sheldon Eisenstein from Bloomington, Indiana" didn't quite have the same sting.)

Do you need a stage name? For some, the decision is easy. Perhaps you bear the same last name as a famous arsonist or genocidal dictator. Maybe your name is actually *too* generic. "Stephanie Smith" won't be capturing the hearts of America and cashing residual checks. She'll be doing cuts and colors out of her kitchen in Boise. Your stage name should be familiar enough to make you seem approachable, but different enough so you're memorable. Jenna Jameson, the most famous porn actress of all time, has the perfect stage name. "Jenna" is fun, American, and young. "Jameson" is a booze, it's classy, and it has an alliteration with "Jenna," which makes it super fun to say. Of course she's stunning and charismatic, but you have to wonder if she could have possibly conquered the porn world without such an amazing moniker.

Choosing a stage name shouldn't be difficult. It should mean something to you, but it should still roll off the tongue and tell your story. When I was picking my drag name, I was lucky enough to get Trixie Mattel out of a Zoltar machine. What luck! I jest. Actually, "Trixie" is an old-school slur for a homosexual man. Originally, I only wanted a one-word name, like "Madonna" or "Cher." Or "Tylenol." But the year was 2009 and Facebook said I had to have a last name in order to create a profile for Trixie. Since "Mattel" is the maker of Barbie, I thought it would make sense as my last name. Luckily it has a nice ring to it, and it seems to have had some life span thus far. I know a lot of drag queens have changed names several times because the first few didn't stick. Or they have multiples! (Did you know Heidi N. Closet's name when she was a disc jockey was

DJ CLOSETCASE?!) RuPaul's first drag name was famously "Bertrude," but she decided it sounded too provocative.

Whatever you choose, you'll know it's right when it comes to you. I remember saying "Trixie Mattel" out loud in my apartment on the east side of Milwaukee and being like, "Excuse me while I snap on all these bitches." I saw lunch boxes, I saw billboards, and I saw myself cashing checks from selling this exact book.

I'm also very lucky because I have yet to encounter any legal issues with Mattel. Luckily I have a near encyclopedic knowledge of Barbie and so I think my reverence for the iconic toy has kept me out of the courtroom. However, every time I get a call from someone at Mattel regarding a PR opportunity or an invite to an event, I am always wondering if it's "the call" that gets my skinny ass sued the house down. In the event that I am sued, I will lean into the royalties from my incredible literary career.

The moral of the story here is to make sure you pick something unique that hasn't been pissed on by someone else already. Example: At this point, between Kylie Minogue, Kylie Jenner, and Kylie Sonique Love, you should really pick something else.

If you're strapped for stage name ideas and you need some inspiration, here are some A-list actresses' real names:

Reese Witherspoon: Martha Fork

Renée Zellweger: Puffy the Clam

Jennifer Aniston: Jenny 867-5309

Catherine Zeta-Jones: Spicy Spicy Lady

Margot Robbie: Tonya Harding

Drew Barrymore: Oprah Winfrey

Cher: Chair

Madonna: Dasani Normani Jenkins

Iggy Azalea: Amethyst Kelly (*This one is real and is so gaggy.*)

HEADSHOTS

I'm going to be honest: I personally went directly from taking my own eight-by-tens in theater school to being a reality TV personality with an extremely memorable face. (I guess you could call what I have in drag a face; it's more like graffiti.) For this reason, I skipped the humiliating and unnavigable waters of headshots. I was spared the endless, spiraling layers of doubt: What am I going to wear? What wig should I wear? How am I going to act? Am I gonna cry?

Luckily for you, the reader, I have two types of developed experience: being horribly ugly out of drag and being a beautiful and heavily photographed persona in drag. I have become somewhat of an authority in catfishing as a beautiful starlet, when in reality I should be in an eye patch working back of house at a restaurant in northeast Wisconsin. I have been able to traverse the world of the rich and stunning because cameras can be much more forgiving than you think.

Most people hate to be photographed, but the truth is that for most of us, a well-lit photo and a little hair and makeup is the best we will ever look. And a strong headshot can be the catalyst to an illustrious showbiz career. Remember that the next time you are trying to be a relatable Gen Z and you're taking Instagram stories as an upshot with no makeup on and a bunch of flyaways.

Here's what your headshot smile says about you:

Closed-mouth smile:

Congratulations. You are a normal human who is relatable. You are allowing the casting director to imagine you fully smiling or pulling back to a pensive stare. You deserve good things and a life, and people find you pleasantly acceptable. Pass Go and collect two hundred dollars because your headshot is doing what it's supposed to do.

"Wacky" one: Oh boy. Once again, a congratulations is in order because you technically have accomplished something. You have successfully convinced anyone in casting that you are not only *not* funny, you are annoying, and you have taken and retaken Improv Level One several times without ever advancing. You are the type of person who believes they have bad luck with roommates when in fact you are a reliable and fast-acting poison in any living situation. You were the lead in a high school musical and you still talk about it. You auditioned for a gig on a cruise ship almost two years ago, but you are "still waiting to hear back." You actually might be right for many types of roles and projects, but we will never find out because your headshot is the equivalent of a limp, poorly lit dick pic.

Serious, sexy smolder: You are a girl who is just shy of being very attractive, but you believe you are literally Megan Fox hot, so it's a turnoff. In fact, your name is probably Megan, but it's pronounced "MEE-gin" and you definitely correct people. If you are a guy doing the serious smolder, you are either a huge fag or a straight guy who has regularly said "fag." You believe if you don't smile whatsoever in the photo, people will believe you're a Daniel Day-Lewis- or Laurie Metcalf-level serious actor. Instead, you look like a graceless turd who needs to lighten up a bit.

AUDITION MATERIAL

If you're new to the game, you're going to need to find and develop two contrasting monologues: usually one comedic and one more dramatic. In college, I had to mine the libraries for audition books full of monologues. Then, if I found something suitable for my type (which is faggy bald fuck), I had to track down the full play and read it for context. After months of coloring in this short-form character performance, I would audition for regional theater companies and literally never hear anything back. I turned to drinking, which turned me on to wigs, which actually worked out for me in the long run. Turns out improv on a green screen in women's clothing was my calling!

For you, I have assembled some suggested audition materials that you, a young thespian, can sink your plastic vampire fangs into:

- *Buyer & Cellar* (this fabulous play about the only employee in Barbra Streisand's basement mall)

- The Cerulean Monologue from *The Devil Wears Prada*

- The Scary Island episode of *RHONY*

- The Sugar Daddy monologue by Miss Shangela Laquifa Wadley

- A Poo-Pourri commercial

- The Tiffany Pollard *Celebrity Big Brother* (UK) "Gemma" confessional

- A Meghan McCain "My Father" rant

- The first fifteen minutes of the movie *Soapdish*

- The Rockette monologue from *A Chorus Line*

- The lyrics to "Disco Inferno" by the Trammps

- Delta Boeing 777 in-flight safety demonstration

- Any passage ever interpreted by Jennifer Coolidge

SCAMS

The Grift That Keeps on Giving

BY KATYA

Scam (n.)—A dishonorable dirty-dealing grift accomplished by swindling unsuspecting suckers

Everybody wants to make money, but few people want to work hard. I'll be the first to admit it, as I am currently dictating this paragraph into my computer while receiving a shiatsu massage. After I finish this sentence, I am going to reward myself with a three-hour nap.

All right, I am back. Wow, that was nice! Where was I again? Oh yes. Working hard for a paycheck has fallen out of fashion, just like wired headphones and Elizabethan collars. In our fast-paced, digital age, consistent hard work has been buried by the algorithm, which favors what I call the Three Fs: fraudulence, forgery, and fucking garbage.

We are far too quick to place our trust in some rando with an official-looking title. For example, my title of *RuPaul's Drag Race All Stars* runner-up has afforded

me enough credibility to write a book about the modern workplace, a subject I have little to no expertise in, and you have enough trust in me to spend your own hard-earned money on it nevertheless. If that makes me a scammer, then lock me up.

The definition of "scam" used to be black-and-white. Either you were selling someone a good or service in exchange for their money, or you weren't. Back before the internet, a scam was a scam, no question. Nobody was arguing that someone who forged paintings was a legitimate small business owner who deserved your support. Nowadays, scammers live and walk among us everywhere. In our modern age, social media wraps up even the most wicked scam in a cloak of trustworthiness. A masked robber breaking into a 7-Eleven with a sawed-off shotgun is undeniably seen as a crook, or, at best, a soldier on the front lines of the class war. Meanwhile, a random person with no health or fitness education shilling radioactive weight-loss shakes on her Instagram is seen as an entrepreneur. Even the most mediocre social media user has the ability to be seen as a trusted spokeswoman for whatever hack product they want to promote to their unwitting followers. Throw on a filter and some trendy typography, and your next grift could get pushed to the top of the algorithm and broadcast to the world.

As someone who has made a career off of illusions and visual trickery, I know that it's easy to begin your grift; the real challenge is maintaining it. When I announced to the world that I was a beautiful, big-breasted, chunky-assed woman with long blond hair, I did not think about the fact that seven years later I would have to continue to pour my time and money into maintaining the image I first presented to the world. Had I come on to *Drag Race* as my other identity, a bald-headed bitch who eats lightbulbs, it would have been much more sustainable in the long run. But would people have fallen in love with Bumpy Bullet the way they did with Katya Zamolodchikova? No, because the illusion of the perfect, delicate, gorgeous young woman is shattered.

Beauty and fitness scams have always relied on the gullibility and cognitive dissonance of the consumer. Your brain wants to believe the candy-colored, factually lacking propaganda from these unreliable sources, because they're so much more alluring than boring, dense "facts." Who cares if nine out of ten dentists recommend flossing, when a TikToker with paper-white teeth was photographed holding a device that whitens your teeth with flashing neon lights? If dentists and other medical professionals want to be listened to, they should consider bleaching the front parts of their hair and doing "the woah." Testimonials for waist trainers that squish your organs together from Instagram models who are fresh from their BBL recovery will always hold our attention more than a sustainable long-term workout plan from a certified personal trainer. These scams prey on your insecurities by telling you that there is an easy, moderately priced solution that you can certainly trust, because it's being endorsed by real people.

Filters exacerbate the perception of our flaws by instantly showing us a reflection who is everything we're not in real life. I have dealt with my own share of self-image issues due to my phone's ability to show me what I would look like if I was a baby. I close my photo app and look in my mirror, devastated to see that I am not actually a baby. I cannot cross paths with an actual infant or toddler, due to the risk that I might impulsively approach them and perform a *Freaky Friday*-style body switch.

Thanks to the sprawling collection of data that the internet has on each of us, scams are constantly trying to infiltrate our digital lives. Fraudsters will stop at nothing to get your attention, whether it's through robocalls or fake emails pretending to be your boss asking for GameStop gift cards. When we all have microchips implanted into our arms someday, they will probably lack the security necessary to prevent us from getting ads for suspiciously priced Ray-Bans. Sorry, but the only chip I will be putting in my body is a potato chip. Yum!

A discipline of the Scamming Arts that is a fixture in pop culture is MLM, which stands for multilevel marketing. MLMs revolve around the recruitment of a workforce who are not only unpaid but also have to buy their inventory themselves in order to begin selling. It's not a real job, but to call it "clownery" would be an insult to all the hardworking individuals of the clown industry. The real money here comes from having "down lines" (aka your hoodwinked recruits), who recruit their own minions too, until you are the kingpin of your shampoo / protein bar / leggings empire. If you do well enough, you may be gifted a large SUV or a trip to Tijuana for bariatric surgery. Most people who enter MLMs leave with less money than they started with, and the stink of a dirty scammer.

MLMs are often mistaken for cults, which have a lot more flair, style, and cultural consciousness. While both MLMs and cults involve manipulation, legal torture, and impressive recruitment tactics, it is critical that you not confuse the two. MLMs have a huge element of perception on social media, with your online following serving as your customer base and your recruitment pool. Cults, meanwhile, tend to exist in shadowy corners, hidden away from society, so they can create their own version of reality. Someone who would be a good fit for an MLM might not do great in a cult, and vice versa.

In our modern age, as people are struggling to afford the rising cost of living, many are desperate for opportunities to make money. This is especially true for parents who might not be able to commit to a full-time office job, or those with an unattractive résumé due to lack of education or a criminal record. My advice to you as you come across opportunities to make money is simple. Two words: MEDIA LITERACY. Use critical thinking to look for red flags.

Let's try it out right here and now! Read the following job listings and see if you can spot the scams.

1. Seeking an administrative assistant for a fast-paced office environment. Starting pay $18–20/hr depending on experience. Please submit a résumé and cover letter via email.

2. Looking for some BOSS BABES looking to start their own beauty business <3. Are you ready to join a group of driven, motivated ladies? Come to this party at an undisclosed location and bring $10,000 in cash.

3. Now hiring a Project Manager with 2–3 years of experience. Must be a team player and comfortable wearing many different hats. Submit a résumé, cover letter, and references below.

4. Do you feel a lack of purpose in your life? Feeling directionless? Do you have type A blood? Please come down to the quarry wearing nothing except a linen sack at nightfall.

5. Looking to hire a part-time cashier to start immediately. Must have availability evenings and weekends. Experience not required. Give us a call or stop in this week for an interview on-site.

6. If you are a gullible person with lots of inherited money, come to the shack made out of discarded shipping pallets behind the abandoned Kmart.

ANSWER KEY:

1. Scam.

2. Scam.

3. Scam.

4. Scam.

5. Scam.

6. I'm not sure about this one. I want to hear them out!

RETIREMENT
AND MORE

You Better Not Work!

BY KATYA

A t this point, this book probably has you thinking, "Wow, the modern workplace is a twisted psychological experiment that should get shut down by the FDA, and all participants should be paid a hefty settlement that ensures their financial future with no question." Welcome, comrade, you are absolutely correct. Your hammer and sickle are in the mail. There is no ethical consumption under capitalism, and even the most enjoyable job munches on you like a leech. You may be so disgusted by this realization that you are tempted to fully extricate yourself from this system by any means necessary.

If you're suddenly looking for a way out, you're not alone. Thousands of people quit their jobs every day. And that's just at Barnes & Noble. In the United States, someone quits their job every millisecond. As you're reading this sentence, at least ten baristas in a half-mile radius are handing in their aprons, badges, and guns. Unfortunately, though, sustainably removing yourself from the workforce is about as easy and painless as removing a full back-tattoo portrait of Loni Anderson. And doing so presents you with just as many questions and crises of conscience. It's a huge commitment, and one where you can't think twice, because you are shutting off your main income source.

While almost everybody wants to stop working, nobody wants to stop being able to pay their bills, except debt fetishists. Assuming you do not find pleasure or arousal in accruing a massive pile of unpaid bills, you need to have your ducks in a row before removing yourself from the workforce. This conundrum is the one that often puzzles people for life and keeps them from acting on their wish to *Eat, Pray, Love* their way out of the rat race.

That being said, there still do exist a few pathways for remission from the inoperable human condition known as employment.

PRE-COLLEGE GAP YEAR

Say you just finished high school, and impending adult responsibilities already have you considering early retirement. Not so fast! The first and easiest way to avoid entering the workplace in your young life is to take a gap year. No, not a year of serving as a living mannequin at your local Gap store. The other gap year, where you take a year off before college.

A gap year is common for new high school grads who want to take an extra year before leaving the nest. Oftentimes, this is a structured year of international travel and voluntourism, like cleaning up lamb shit in New Zealand. Now that college is basically a million dollars a semester, if you don't know what you want to get your degree in, it is actually very economical to take a year or two to figure out who you are and what you want.

The belief system behind the gap year is one we can all get behind: You shouldn't throw yourself headfirst into the professional pipeline just because society tells you it's time. Big decisions, like college, jobs, and haircuts, should all be driven by genuine desire, not societal pressure.

If you aren't someone who just finished high school, you should feel free to create your own gap year by just running into the woods under the cover of night. You may return twelve months later fully rejuvenated and ready for freshman seminar at Penn State.

ACADEMIC
SABBATICAL

In academic spaces, all new experiences are forms of professional development. When your occupation deals with talking about the world, it's ideal that you know more about that world, right? Reading and writing can only show you a few sides of the dodecahedron that is our society. Academic excellence hinges on a wide variety of perspectives, all jousting with each other in the arena that is the lecture hall. If I were a university faculty member, this is exactly how I would hustle for sabbatical, except with more usage of words like "modernity" and "contemporary modes of intersectional discourse."

Sabbatical affords you a semester or two of paid time off to do whatever you want as long as you can justify it making you a more valuable member of your department at the university. Every professor comes back from

201

sabbatical looking hot and tight and practically radiating tranquility. Sometimes they also come back having written a book, or an article to be published in an academic journal. But other times they just come back with a new international lover or a nose piercing. Regardless, it's a period of personal growth and development that we all deserve.

To set yourself up as the MVP (Most Valuable Professor), I would suggest specializing in a very niche subject and becoming the resident expert of it to make yourself extra appealing to a university. Then start some drama in the academic literati community and wait until you become an infamous cult-favorite intellectual provocateur who will draw brainy prospective students to their school in droves. Become the next Foucault, but make it hot and sexy. Some ideas for your thesis: "The Male Gaze and Erotic Pleasure of *Riverdale*," "Aries/Capricorn Compatibility and Its Effects on the Tides," or "Jennifer Lawrence." You will achieve universal acclaim as a great modern thinker, and some stuffy college with a yearly endowment bigger than the GDP of Panama will make you an offer you can't refuse. Show up to campus with an iconic, highly accessorized wardrobe that makes you an easily recognizable fixture, and speak in dense, intellectual jargon that confuses and lures your students and colleagues. These tips will catapult you to sabbatical in no time.

CORPORATE LEAVE OF ABSENCE

The advantage of working a corporate job is the robust benefits package that accompanies your offer of employment. Included in that package is a paid-leave policy. While sometimes that policy is "Nothing, sorry!" you could also be in a position to receive temporary paid leave from your employer. It's true! It's vital that you, as an employee, know your rights to scam, scheme, and scrooge your way to time off.

One way to get some paid vacation time is to have a baby. As the United States does not have federally mandated paid family leave, and most states have very little to offer beyond that, the real money is in international child-rearing.

Countries like Sweden and Finland are best known for their strong offerings for new families, but don't look past Eastern European countries like Serbia and Estonia, either.

Make sure your passport is up-to-date, then go off to one of these countries and take a lover who wants to join you in starting a family. Or, hey, make it a real excursion and see how many different countries with strong family leave policies you can make love in. This opens up the door to you having a beautiful multicultural tapestry of a family à la the erstwhile Jolie-Pitts, or a *Mamma Mia!*–type situation in the future. Either way, it's evocative of Hollywood and therefore very chic. You could get eight-plus months of paid leave all for the small price of bringing another human into the world and then raising them for eighteen-plus years. An easy trade-off.

If your desire to sloth is not dependent on stable income, might I also suggest:

- **Rehab:** If you can afford the eye-popping price tag, you can expect countless amenities, tons of opportunities to make art, and friends for life. It's just like in the movies, but even better. If you are not suffering with a disease that requires inpatient treatment, "exhaustion" is a safe reason for admission.

- **Go on strike:** Gather your coworkers and collectively bargain by withholding your labor until your needs are met. If you love making signs/T-shirts or writing chants, this one is a great opportunity to express your creativity. Unions rule! Every workplace could be improved, but off the top of my head, you could bargain for: higher wages, overtime, stronger benefits, HR, more structured scheduling, the dismissal of a harasser, reimbursed public transit costs, or even your team's own personal wishes, like for pony rides in the lobby or to put Tom from Accounting in a dunk tank. Needless to say, there is strength in numbers, and you shouldn't give up until all your desires are met.

- **Fake your disappearance/death:** Pretty self-explanatory. But you must have your story straight. Here's a sample chain of events.

  - *Thursday:* Tell everyone you're taking Friday off and going "upstate" for the weekend. Don't explain why.

  - *Friday:* Leave your apartment haphazardly cluttered, with a few planted items to create an air of mystery for any investigators. Then throw your phone into a sewer grate.

  - *Saturday:* Hop on a train to Akron (pay cash!), change your name, and enjoy the first day of the rest of your life.

SPECIAL CIRCUMSTANCES

This one doesn't apply to most people, but if you find yourself becoming a C-suite executive at a corporation that is undergoing a merger, you might end up with what is known as a "golden parachute," or a guaranteed payout should you be dismissed as a result of the merger. Though opportunities like this are rare, they are incredibly lucrative, so here is my advice:

1. Find a large corporation that lives on the edge and is filled with a ton of character and dueling personalities, ideally one that is a star on the rise. Look for some sort of tech company that was started by two stoners who were roommates at Stanford, or an ominous venture capital group whose name sounds like a *Batman* villain.

2. Work your way up from the bottom to the boardroom, where you are respected and revered but seen as a bit of a wild card. As your star rises along with the company's, this will put you within arm's reach of a contract with a golden parachute.

3. Once the ink has dried on your contract, steer the company toward a merger with a more established competitor that is your

corp's style opposite—a traditional, stuffy company that can't afford a loose cannon like you. On the first day of the merger, drive this message home by dressing like you're on Fire Island and making a risky suggestion during a senior meeting. Perhaps this involves data mining or the illegal arms trade. Make your ringtone something by Pitbull and have someone call your phone during the meeting. This combination of liabilities will be your career's kiss of death and hook you up with that sweet, sweet dinero.

RETIREMENT

The idea of retirement is seductive: You're likely frothing at the mouth at the idea of removing yourself from the Sisyphean charade of work to run over the feet of your enemies with an electric scooter at the grocery store. We as a society can't wait to trade in company-wide meetings and profit reports for midmorning tennis and light Jazzercise. Being a retiree, especially in the sixty-two-plus age range, is associated with several special privileges: discount coffee, a subscription to the glossy pages of *AARP the Magazine*, and being able to say whatever the fuck you want because you've been alive for a long time. Also, it's crucial to note that retirement communities are a flashing-red hot spot on the horniness index. Retiring is a great option for revitalizing your sex life, and an excellent way to catch gonorrhea.

Being a retiree, much like being a toddler, often includes a full agenda of low-impact recreational activities. For example, a Tuesday being "fully booked" could mean 11:00 a.m. water aerobics, 1:00 p.m. book club, and a 3:30 p.m. dinner with the girls, then calling it a day. And, if you're that kind of girl, a few sexual escapades here and there.

Sounds amazing, right? But the truth is, unless you're a greyhound past your glorious racing days or are on your fourth tech startup, you may not find retirement easy. Employer pensions and social security do not go as far as they used to,

and the cost of living has risen greatly across the country. Experts suggest that you start saving for retirement by your mid-twenties, and that words like "401(k)" and "Roth IRA" enter your vocabulary before you're old enough to rent a car. In my case, I didn't have any money in my savings account until I got on TV at thirty-two. Because it relies on a lifetime of high financial literacy and a strong foundation of savings or a lucky stream of high income, a retirement full of leisurely activities and free of worry is usually reserved for the bourgeoisie. It's especially elusive to gay people, who largely will not have adult children that they can impose themselves on in their old age.

For these reasons, I can only give this piece of retirement advice, which appeared on my mirror written in blood one morning: A great method to save money is to use your youth while you have it. Suck and fuck as much as you can now and put away the coins for your future retirement fund, so you can suck and fuck even more in the comfort of an upper-middle-class retirement community. Or, I guess, you could be incredibly frugal and

penny-pinching your entire life. But if you spent your own hard-earned money on this book, I can only assume you are not that kind of person.

As I enter my forties, I come closer and closer to the possibility that my life will not end as I had once hoped: in a fiery car crash inside a shopping mall. So I've been putting away plenty of cash to save for the unthinkable: living past the age of sixty. I've got some great role models for this stage of life, as my grandparents were vibrant and active right until their last breaths. My grandmother showed me that just because you don't work anymore doesn't mean you can't continue to "*work it, diva.*" And that "it" could be any number of things, like nursing a secret gambling addiction or a thorough exploration of late-in-life lesbianism.

So whether you are lucky enough to make it through the modern workplace with your sanity intact and your finances fat and chunky, or you're one of the unfortunate many who must toil mercilessly until the bitter end and you wheeze out your last malnourished breath while stocking beef soup cans at the Piggly Wiggly—we sincerely hope that you were able to locate somewhere in this relentlessly unhelpful guidebook at least one or two fragments of useful advice. And when you inevitably breach the summit of your field, breathless and bleary-eyed, there's no need to thank us—all we ask is that you maintain a shred of compassion for all those unfortunate workers whose necks you trampled and gouged with your five-inch stilettos on your way up. Remember, it doesn't matter how lofty or mundane your goals may be. It doesn't matter if you graduate from Harvard and recover all the missing gold from WWII, or if your thighs and back flesh slowly graft onto the upholstery of a halfway house pullout couch—we're all still people who deserve respect, dignity, a living wage, and a sickening supply of Anastasia Beverly Hills cosmetics. So go out there and show those bony bitches just how fiercely a true dog diva can howl.

ACKNOWL

TRIXIE

I would like to thank: David Silver; my family; Katya Zamolodchikova; Brandon Lim; Eden Friedman; Albert Sanchez and Pedro Zalba; David Charpentier, Jacob Slane, and everyone at PEG; Marya Pasciuto and everyone at Plume.

EDGMENTS

KATYA

There are so many wonderful, talented people who contributed to the creation of this very important book. In no particular order, I would like to thank Albert Sanchez, Pedro Zalba, David Charpentier, Jacob Slane, Marya Pasciuto, Jill Schwartzman, Alice Dalrymple, Shannon Plunkett, Susan Schwartz, Laura Rosenblum, Jamie Knapp, Becky Odell, Isabel DaSilva, Jason Booher, Christopher Lin, Ryan Carpenter, Andrew Yang, Maddie Jacobs, Tom Flannery, Melanie Griffith, Julia Roberts, Christina Applegate, Sigourney Weaver, Harrison Ford, Sharon Stone, Octavia Spencer, Ma and her gravy, Karen Susinksi, Maggie Rosenthal, my lovely family. And last, but certainly not least—in fact, first and foremost—an extra special thanks to the inimitable and incomparable Eden Ruth Friedman.

ABOUT THE

Trixie Mattel
is a drag performer, singer-songwriter, and comedian. She
loves personal achievement and the movie *Jawbreaker*.

AUTHORS

Katya Zamolodchikova

is a woman in her early forties looking to fall in love in the next three to five weeks. She lives in Los Angeles with her ex-husband, Glen, and her four beautiful daughters. This is her second book.

Until next time, goodbye!